DESERT HOUSE

By

SAMUEL T. CARSON

AMBASSADOR

ISBN 1 898787 05 0

AMBASSADOR PRODUCTIONS LTD
Providence House,
16 Hillview Avenue,
Belfast, BT5 6JR
U.K.

Printed by GNBA Design & Print
Bawtry Hall, Bawtry, Doncaster (0302) 710576

Dedication:

To father and mother and sister Martie, all of whom are now with the Lord. It was through their conversation, during my formative years at home, that my heart first warmed to those scriptures which are the basis of this book.

Acknowledgements

The photographs used in this book are taken from the Marshall Model of the Tabernacle, and are used with the kind permission of the Myrtlefield Trust.

Line Drawing on Page 12 by Brian McCrum.

Contents

Part 3

The Entrance Hall

Part 4

The Private Apartment

Part 5

Foreword

In the introduction to this book the author uses the word 'neglected' in referring to the subject matter that follows. Any part of God's word which is neglected leads to spiritual impoverishment.   When the Apostle Paul wrote to Timothy he wisely reminded him that, 'all scripture is given by inspiration ... and is profitable ... ' (2Tim.3:16). Teaching on the Tabernacle has not been given high priority of recent years and I am glad therefore that Sam Carson has given us such a splendid little book.

The plans and blueprints of all God's work begin with Himself. However, the implementing of those plans involves people. The 'Desert House' or Tabernacle is one such example. God commanded and Moses executed those instructions. Blessing followed as God's glory filled that special house in the desert. Obedience always leads to blessing.

We cannot overemphasize the teaching of the cross and the centrality of the Saviour. Sam Carson brings everything beautifully into focus as he opens up and teaches the meaning of, and the underlying reasons for, God's 'Desert House'.

You will read this book with profit and pleasure.

David Oram.
Radio Bible Teacher.
Good News Broadcasting Association.

Introduction

We believe and are sure that all scripture is given by inspiration of God and is profitable. This is equally true of both Old and New Testaments. In practice, however, we often convey an altogether different impression. Large tracts, especially of the Old Testament are seldom discussed and some are almost entirely neglected.

A case in point is that section of scripture beginning with Exodus chapter 25 and running through to Leviticus chapter 9. Here we have a most wonderful and divinely given object lesson in three parts; (1) The Tabernacle (2) The Priesthood and (3) The Offerings. The church of Christ has without doubt been greatly impoverished by the neglect of these things which were written for our learning.

This threefold object lesson is given to us against the background of a redeemed people. Having been brought under the blood (Ex.12) and then through the sea (Ex.14) Israel's first thought was of a house for the Lord. "I will build Him a habitation." (Ex.15:2) The thought itself was from God and it found its visible expression in the Tabernacle.

The House of God

The house of God in Old Testament times was firstly the Tabernacle in the wilderness and then the Temple in the land. But in this age God's house is a spiritual building and not material. The house of God to-day is the Church, composed of believers who are built upon Christ, the living stone, and who themselves are living stones through the regenerating work of the Holy Spirit.

Often referred to as the Church universal, this body of Christ is expressed locally in local fellowships of believers. This means that in practical terms, our house of God is our local church, just as in the wilderness, Israel's house of God was the Tabernacle. We have our buildings set aside for the worship and service of God, but He does not dwell in any of them; He dwells in the spiritual temple which is His people. He indwells the Church by His Spirit, and He does so by indwelling each individual member of it.

Our warrant for studying the Tabernacle is first general and then specific and both are firmly grounded in the New Testament. First, Paul insists that Israel's wilderness experiences happened to them by way of example to us, and have been recorded for our admonition. (See 1Cor.10:11.)

And then the writer of the epistle to the Hebrews tells us that the Tabernacle was an example and shadow of heavenly things. (See Hebs.8:5, 9:11, 10:1.) Indeed he goes so far as to point out that he could have expounded all the Tabernacle details, and not simply the one or two features that were relevant to his immediate argument. (Hebs.9:5)

The Holy Spirit alone can guide us into all truth. It follows that in reading both Testaments we must maintain a constant awareness of our dependence on the Spirit's illuminating ministry, and carefully compare scripture with scripture. It would be beyond our present range to investigate the use that the New Testament makes of the Old: at the same time we cannot forget the well worn truism usually attributed to St Augustine,

> "The New is in the Old contained;
> The Old is by the New explained."

Unbridled imagination may lead to unwarranted deductions which in the end will not profit the Church of God. However, to use such a possibility as a pretext for the wholesale abandonment of large tracts of scripture is a grave negligence, the pernicious influence of which must, in the end impoverish us all.

The New Testament gives us our title to explore the broad expanses of Old Testament scripture, and to gather there comfort and instruction for our souls. The title is clear and plain, it says, "Whatsoever things were written aforetime were written for our learning, that we through patience and comfort of the scriptures might have hope." (Rom.15:1) With these things carefully borne in mind, our intention is to proceed, humbly, to explore the Tabernacle in the wilderness which we are calling 'Desert House'.

A threefold drawing

The Tabernacle is a threefold illustration. First it speaks of heaven, then of the person of our Lord Jesus Christ, and lastly of the Church, the mystical body of Christ. The entry of Israel's High Priest on the great day of atonement into the most holy place found its answer and fulfilment in the entry of Christ, our Great High Priest, into heaven itself. "For Christ is not entered into the holy places made with hands, which are a figure of the true; but into heaven itself, now to appear in the presence of God for us." (Hebs. 9:24)

God's initial instruction to Moses was, "let them make me a sanctuary that I may dwell among them." (Ex. 25:8) We know that God dwells in the heavens above and that He indwells the Church on earth. He also tabernacled in the humanity of our Lord Jesus Christ. (John 1:14) It is to Him that the Tabernacle primarily points. Of the Temple it was said, "everything utters His glory." The same may be said of the Tabernacle in the wilderness: every facet of it declares the Saviour's grace and glory.

The outer court or quadrangle of the Tabernacle had an unbroken wall of fine twined linen, suspended upon sixty pillars. These pillars were joined one to another by silver bands, making one frame. As the sixty pillars made just one frame, so the many believers comprise the one 'body of Christ'. The same idea may be seen in the superstructure of the Tabernacle proper. There were forty-eight boards each encased in gold. Each board, overlaid with gold, speaks of the Christian as 'a man in Christ'. But these boards were joined together by bars to form one Tabernacle. Many boards but just one Tabernacle: many Christians but just one Church of Christ. Thus the Tabernacle in certain senses symbolises the Church.

Our purpose is to major on the second and third of these three ways in which the Tabernacle may be viewed. We shall see here wondrous pictures of Christ personal. Unique insights will present themselves of Him "of whom Moses in the law, and the prophets did write." At the same time other details will be seen which find their proper answer in Christ Mystical; that is to say, in Christ and the Church, His mystical body.

A heavenly pattern

The Tabernacle is detailed for us in two distinct ways. The first begins in the most holy place with the ark and the mercy seat and proceeds outwards to the gate of the court; the other begins without and proceeds inwards to the presence of God. The whole story of our redemption is illustrated in this twofold approach to the Tabernacle. Redemption is the story of how our glorious Redeemer came out from God in order that He might bring us back to God.

Time and again in receiving the Tabernacle details, Moses was exhorted to ensure that all was done according to the pattern shown to him on the mount. The last chapter of the book of Exodus repeatedly emphasises that when eventually all was complete and the Tabernacle was set up it was exactly as the Lord had commanded.

This great principle of complete subjection to the revealed will of God which undergirded the construction of the Tabernacle, needs to be reasserted in our day. God's will is done in heaven; it was done in every step of our Saviour's walk through this world and it will be done throughout the earth in a coming day. In the meantime it is to be done in the hearts of all who love our Lord Jesus Christ in sincerity and in truth. Thus the Tabernacle proclaims the glory that is Christ's and it shows how He is to be glorified in His people.

PART ONE

The Quadrangle

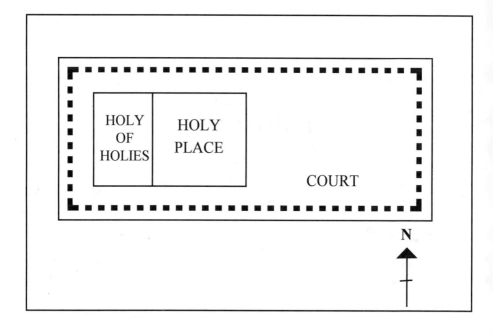

Scripture Reference
Exodus 27:9-19
38:9-20

The Quadrangle

The sanctuary in which God dwelt among His people during their wilderness wanderings, was called the Tabernacle. It was pitched whenever they encamped and the tribes pitched their tents around it. After the people entered Caanan under Joshua, the Tabernacle was set up first at Shiloh (Josh.18:1), and later at Gibeon (1Chron.16:39). Eventually the Ark of the covenant, which was the centrepiece of the Tabernacle, found its permanent resting place in the Temple of Solomon. (1Kings 8:1-4)

The Tabernacle was called the 'tent of meeting' because it was a tent-like structure and it was the appointed meeting place between God and His people. God had said to Moses, "let them make me a sanctuary, that I may dwell among them." (Ex. 25:8)

The Tabernacle was in three clearly defined parts. What we shall call the Tabernacle proper was divided into two. The first part was known as the Holy Place and the second as the Most Holy Place. The third part was the enclosure around the Tabernacle proper. This outer Quadrangle was known as the Court.

The Court was 100 cubits long and 50 cubits wide. (a cubit is usually taken to be about 18 inches) It had no covering, save the heavens; and the desert sand was its floor. Around its perimeter stood 60 pillars upon sockets of brass: twenty pillars for each of the long sides and ten pillars for each of the short sides. Five cubits of fine twined linen were visible between each pillar. This white linen wall formed an unbroken enclosure, except at the east side where the Gate was suspended upon its four pillars.

The different features of the Quadrangle are worthy of individual consideration; but we shall simply mention them at this stage since we intend dealing with them each in turn. They were as follows,

The Furnishings

These were three in number. There was first the Gate of entrance which points to the Lord Jesus who said, "I am the way... no man comes to the Father but by me". (John 14:6) Immediately within the Gate stood the Altar of brass (probably bronze or copper) which in many wonderful ways, as we shall see, speaks of the work of the cross. Finally there was the Laver which teaches us our need of practical, daily cleansing from the defiling effect of sin in our lives.

The Hangings

The hangings or outer curtain which formed the perimeter wall of the Quadrangle were of fine twined linen. Scripture clearly identifies the linen as a symbol of the righteousness of the saints. In the Tabernacle it refers to God's righteousness. It also speaks of the righteousness of the saints (See Rev. 19:8). Two superlative expressions of God's righteousness are given us in His word: the law of Moses in the Old Testament, and the life of Christ in the New. The very whiteness of the hangings, as well as the fineness of their texture, may profitably be thought of as expressing that righteousness which was seen in its fulness in our Lord Jesus Christ. "who did no sin, neither was guile found in His mouth".

The hangings had the practical effect of dividing between those within and those without. Before God, every person occupies one of two positions: either we are 'without Christ' or we are 'in Christ'. "At that time you were without Christ ... but now in Christ..." (Eph 2:12,13) It follows that our position before God is determined by how we stand in relation to the Lord Jesus Christ. It is grace that makes the difference, "for we are saved by grace, through faith alone in Christ. (See Eph. 2:8,9.)

The unbroken wall surrounding the Quadrangle made necessary a way of access. The divinely appointed way was the Gate, positioned at the short eastern side of the enclosure. Just as an Israelite could only draw near to God through the Gate: so it is only through Christ that we can draw near, for He has said, "no man comes to the Father but by me." (John 14:6)

ON THE INSIDE

Having entered through the Gate, the Israelite might have had three things impressed upon his mind.

Firstly, a sense of security.   The linen wall that had shut him out, now shut him in.

Secondly, a sense of sanctity. The very whiteness and fineness of the enclosure proclaimed that holiness becomes God's house.

And thirdly, a sense of separation.   That enclosure was the line of demarcation between those within and those without. God still puts a difference between the righteous and the unrighteous; between those who are in Christ and those who are not. (See Psa.1:1.)

The Gate of the Court (Christ Personal)

Being the only way into the Tabernacle, the Gate speaks eloquently of Him who said, "I am the door; by me if any man enter in he shall be saved." (John 10:9) And again, "I am the way ... no man comes to the Father but by me." (John 14:6) All must have remained outside unless they came by the Gate. In the same way, Christ is not just a Saviour; He is the only Saviour. "There is no other name under heaven given among men, whereby we must be saved." (Acts 4:12) That it teaches man the way to God, is probably the principal lesson to be gleaned from the Tabernacle.

The Gate was four times as long as it was high. It was suspended upon four pillars and it displayed four colours. Four is the universal number: there are four seasons, four elements, four kingdoms and four points on the compass. The gospel of Christ is not limited by race or religion, by class or colour. It is universal in its appeal. Christ is the only Saviour, for the whole world. His invitation is to-day, as of old, "Look unto me, and be saved, all the ends of the earth; for I am God, and there is none else." (Isa.45:22)

ON THE EAST SIDE

Besides its numerical significance, the very position of the Gate seems also to have been significant. It was located at the east side of the Tabernacle. (Ex.28:13-15) Remarkably, it is to the east that men increasingly look for their religion to-day. But in bibical terms the east is the place of man's estrangement, for it was at the east of the garden of Eden that our first parents were driven out from the presence of God. (See Gen 3:24.) And then, when Christ was born, it was from the east that the wise men came in search of Him. The Gate positioned at the east of the Tabernacle serves as a further pointer to Christ as the estranged sinner's only way back to God.

The colours woven into the fabric of the Gate made it a thing of exquisite beauty. The blue, purple and scarlet together with the white of the linen made four colours in all. Scripture does not specify the precise meaning of the various colours, and able expositors sometimes vary in their interpretations of them. Because of this, we have no wish to press our understanding of them beyond measure.

Having said that, however, it is fairly generally agreed that the four colours, can be identified with the four evangelists chosen by God to record the birth, life, death and rising again of our Lord Jesus Christ. Their records combine to give us a marvellous presentation of our wonderful Saviour from four different perspectives.

THE COLOURS

Purple is the royal colour. Leaving aside all the many Tabernacle references to purple, it is first mentioned in scripture in connection with the kings of Midian (Jud.8:26): and Daniel and Mordecai were arrayed in purple robes when they stood before their respective kings. Two of the evangelists record how the soldiers derided the Lord Jesus by putting on Him a purple robe and saying, "Hail king of the Jews!" (See John 19:1-3 & Mark 15:16-18.) On the fact that Matthew speaks of a scarlet robe, most commentators seem to think that the garment was probably a soldiers scarlet cape, faded to resemble royal purple.

In the Tabernacle the purple seems to answer to Matthew's portrayal of Christ in His royalty as God's King. Matthew begins with the question, "where is He that is born King of the Jews?" (Matt.2:2) and ends with a royal proclamation, all the trumpets sounding, and the King being heard to say, "all power is given unto me in heaven and on earth." (Matt.28:18)

The word translated scarlet, is also translated worm in the twenty-second Psalm. In this Psalm Messiah is heard to say, "But I am a worm and no man". (Psa.22:6) The word might even be rendered 'worm-scarlet'. Since the worm is the meanest of God's creatures, the scarlet suggests the second gospel in which Mark presents the Lord Jesus in His humility as God's Servant.

It is the ministry of a servant that is important rather than his genealogy, hence Mark, unlike Matthew and Luke, passes over the geneology of Christ and immediately begins his record with the Saviour's entry upon

His public ministry. This Servant character of our Lord can be traced all through the second gospel, even to the last verse where He is found still active in the service of His God. Although taken up from the apostles, He is said to be still "working with them." (See Mk. 16:19,20.)

Luke, in the third gospel, brings the Lord Jesus before us in His humanity as God's Man. As already observed the very whiteness of the linen as well as the fineness of its texture seem to proclaim the uniqueness of Christ as the perfect man. We are indebted to Luke for practically all we know of the Saviour's babyhood and boyhood. Being a doctor as well as an author, Luke would naturally have an interest in each stage in the life of his subject. Only Luke reports the risen Lord Jesus saying to His disciples, "handle me and see"; Luke was writing of a real man. A man who was tempted and tried as we are, yet without sin.

Blue is the colour of the heavens, and would appear to speak of Christ as John does in the fourth gospel. John emphasises our Saviour's deity as God's Son. John could not be more explicit, he states so plainly his purpose in writing, "that you might believe that Jesus is the Christ, the Son of God; and that believing you might have life through His name." (John 20:31) All the colours in the Gate of the court combine to exalt the Saviour's name. They lead us to say, "He is the chiefest among ten thousand, the altogether lovely."

WHOSOEVER WILL LET HIM COME.

Before concluding, we must call attention to the largeness of the Gate. It was twenty cubits wide, four times as wide as it was high. Truly, "there's a wideness to God's mercy like the wideness of the sea". The gospel of God's grace in Christ is so wondrously broad in its embrace. Consider:

(i) How large the provision grace has made (1 Tim. 2:5,6)

(ii) How large the commission grace has given (Mk. 16:15)

(iii) How large the invitation grace has extended (Rev.22:17).

In marvellous grace God has devised means whereby 'His banished ones need not be expelled from Him forever.' There is a way back to God; and Christ Himself is that way. The gate of mercy stands open for all so that all are without excuse.

The Pillars of the Court (Christ Mystical)

Just as the Gate speaks of Christ Personal, so it is helpful to think of the pillars in terms of Christ Mystical, i.e. of Christ and His people. The many pillars - there were sixty in all - were joined one to another, and so together they formed one frame. The pillars were linked to each other by silver bands. This illustrates the way in which the multitude of believers are one body in the Lord. It is by individual and personal faith in the Lord Jesus that sinners are saved. Yet no one is saved in isolation. Upon our faith in Christ we are not only born again into God's family, we are also incorporated into Christ; we become one with Him by being joined to the Lord as members of His body.

THE UNITY OF THE SPIRIT

Christians, therefore, are not just a collection of individuals; they are members one of another, and members together in the body of Christ. Together they form the universal Church which is sometimes spoken of as Christ Mystical. (See 1.Cor.12:12.)

> many members but just one body.
> many stones but just one building.
> many sheep but just one flock of Jesus.

Several other things are suggested to us by the pillars. Among them we might consider,

1. The pillars did not stand upon the desert sand but on sockets of brass (probably bronze or copper). In the same way believers stand before God, not on the ground of what they might appear to be by nature, but solely on the merit of Christ's vicarious sufferings on the cross. But here we anticipate our next chapter when we shall consider the meaning of the brass.

2. The function of the pillars was to display the hangings. Peter gives us the meaning of this; he exhorts us to "shew forth the praises of Him who has called us out of darkness into His marvellous light". (1Pet.2:9) Not one of us is capable of fully exhibiting Christ. But God's mind is that all of us together should present a complete testimony to Him.

3. The pillars were kept in position by pins and cords. It might be helpful to think of the pins as representing the promises of God, and the cords the faith that lays hold of the promises. As the pillars were thus held fast midst every desert storm, so faith, the faith that takes God at His word, is the victory that enables the believer to overcome in the storms of life. "This is the victory that overcomes the world, even your faith." (1 John 5:4) to God; and Christ Himself is that way. The gate of mercy stands open for all so that all are without excuse.

The Altar of Sacrifice

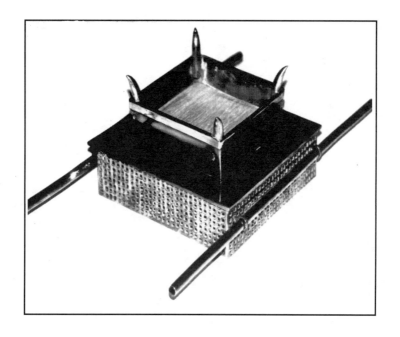

Scripture Reference
Exodus 27:1-8
38:1-7

The Altar of Sacrifice

Stepping through the gate of the Quadrangle we are immediately confronted with the Brazen Altar, sometimes called the altar of burnt offering. Having already seen the person of Christ in the Gate, we shall now see the work of Christ in the Altar. John the Baptist's testimony to Christ was two-fold: witnessing first to the person of Christ, he cried, "Behold the Lamb of God", and then secondly, to the work of Christ, he added, "who takes away the sin of the world." (John 1:29)

The Brazen Altar was the basis of the entire Levitical system. It was the place of sacrifice and it speaks to us of the cross; i.e. of Jesus Christ and Him crucified. However dimly it may be perceived, the cross is the only sure foundation of true faith in God. Men of faith in ages past looked forward and saw the cross; in this age we look back to the cross, and so we speak of the centrality of the cross.

THE MEANING OF THE CROSS

The Altar Materials

The Altar was made of wood and overlaid with brass. The significance of these materials should not be overlooked.   The wood speaks of His humanity, He is the man Christ Jesus. The particular wood used was called shittim or acacia wood. This wood was noted for its durability. The Septuagint actually translates the phrase 'incorruptible wood': and this immediately suggests to us thoughts of the incorruptibility of the human body of our Lord Jesus Christ. (See Acts 2:24-32.)

The Authorised Version consistently speaks of brass but the metal referred to was probably bronze or copper. It is frequently used in scripture to denote what can endure pressure and testing and as seen in the Altar of brass it seems to point to Christ as the one who endured the cross. The primary symbolism of brass seems to be judgement. The serpent of brass (See Num.21:9.) is a prominent type of Christ made sin for us: and when the risen Christ was seen walking in the midst of the churches, evaluating and judging, His feet were said to be of fine brass. (Rev.1:15 & 2:18)

The Altar overlaid with brass causes us to think of how the judgement, due to us, fell upon Christ when "He was wounded for our transgressions, and bruised for our iniquities". (Isa.53:5)

The Altar Measurements

The meaning of the cross is also told out in the measurements of the Altar. It was five cubits by five cubits by three cubits. Three, of course, is the number of God Himself, for there are three persons in the Godhead. The number three is also indelibly stamped upon the cross. It was the third hour of the day when our Saviour was lifted up upon the tree. The darkness lasted for three hours and the inscription over the cross was in three languages.

Three is the number of God and its place in the Altar of burnt offering surely testifies to the hidden side of Calvary and to the truth that "salvation is of the Lord". Atonement was not made by anything that men did to Christ, but by what God did when "He made Him to be sin for us, that we might be made the righteousness of God in Him". (2Cor.5:21)

The number five has its own special significance as well. Five seems to be connected with the thought of God's grace. The word abundant occurs for the first time in the Bible on the fifth day of creation week. The fish of the sea, the beasts of the field and the birds of the air were to bring forth abundantly. Paul said of the cross, "where sin abounded, grace did much more abound." (Rom.5:20) Truly, the grace of God is greater than all our sin. At the very place where sin reached its high water mark, there the grace of God 'superabounded'. The real meaning of the cross can only be appreciated when understood in terms of God and His grace.

THE MESSAGE OF THE CROSS

Its Size

This is first seen in the size of the Altar. It was large enough to contain within itself all the other vessels of the Tabernacle. In the same way, every benefit that divine grace can bestow upon believing sinners is secured and treasured up in the person of Jesus Christ, our crucified but now risen Saviour. We are "blessed with all spiritual blessings in heavenly places in Christ." (Eph.1:3) Whoever the person or whatever the need, 'Christ is the answer.'

Its Shape

The altar was foursquare; it was the same on all sides. Its very shape has an important message for us. It teaches that while there is 'no difference' in that all have sinned there is also 'no difference' in that "the same Lord over all is rich unto all who call upon Him. For whosoever shall call upon the name of the Lord shall be saved". (Rom.10: 12,13)

Its Situation

Another striking feature of the Altar was its situation, it stood immediately before the Gate. The Gate was open at all times and for all people. Approach was always possible. The benefits of the Altar, however, were limited to those who came by way of the Gate. In the same way salvation is universal in its invitation, but only those who believe the gospel will be saved.

Its Sacrifices

We must not overlook the sacrifices that were offered upon the Altar. Of these, the chief sacrifice was the burnt offering. Indeed, the Altar often took its name from this particular sacrifice. The burnt offering was the offering of consecration. It represents the Lord Jesus, pursuing the will of God, in all His ways. It was the pursuit of God's will that led Him all the way to Calvary. "He was obedient unto death, even the death of the cross." (Phil.2:8)

The preaching of the cross is the good news that there was one who was willing to die in our stead, and who, by His death has made atonement for our sin. But the benefits of that atonement are not the portion of all. They are only laid to the account of those who come to Him in faith, and such find in Him their all in all.

THE MYSTERY OF THE CROSS

The Altar had a hollow centre in which there was a grate, one and a half cubits high. Remarkably this was also the precise height of the mercy seat, sometimes spoken of as the throne of God. It may be that we have in this a suggestion of the great truth that the death of Christ was the only sacrifice capable of reaching up to the demands of God's throne. When Jesus, on the cross, cried out "it is finished," God saw that it was enough, and set His seal to the sufficiency of Christ's sacrifice by raising Him from the dead on the third day.

On the corners of the Altar were four horns, symbolising strength and power. Throughout the book of Daniel the 'horn' is used as the emblem of political power in the earth. (See Dan.7&8.) The horns on the Brazen Altar seem to point to Him in whom 'all power in heaven and on earth' is vested.

Speaking of life itself, none but Christ could ever say, "I have power to lay down my life, and I have power to take it again." (John 10:18) This

He did in death upon the cross, for He bowed His head and delivered up His spirit. And then in resurrection He took it again, stepping from the tomb in the power of an endless life. Jesus Christ really died and really rose again from the dead.

He arose, hallelujah, Christ arose.

The Altar Carried

As the people of Israel journeyed through the wilderness, the Altar was carried by means of the staves which passed through the four rings on its sides. The rings, symbols of constant love, and the staves might speak of the love that carried our Saviour through this world and on through the suffering and death of the cross.

Twas love that sought Gethsemane
Or Judas ne'er had found Him.
Twas love that held Him to the tree
Or iron ne'er had bound Him.

It was in the cross that the whole law, as summarised in the two parts of the first commandment, found its supreme and perfect fulfilment in love to God and man.

The Altar Covered

As the Brazen Altar was moved from place to place through the wilderness, it was covered with a covering of purple. We have already identified purple as the kingly colour, the colour of the sovereign. The covering over the Altar tells of 'sovereign grace'. Because of Calvary, where sin abounded, but where grace did much more abound, "grace now reigns through righteousness."(Rom.5:21) We cannot profess to comprehend this mystery; but in beholding our Saviour in the Brazen Altar, may we not in some measure say, "we know the grace of our Lord Jesus Christ." (2 Cor.8:9)

The Laver of Cleansing

Scripture Reference
Exodus 30:17-21
38:8

The Laver Of Cleansing

The Laver was made of brass (probably bronze or copper as in the brazen altar) and as the name suggests it was used for washing. The text speaks of 'the laver ... and the foot of it' and some have inferred from this that it had a lower part for foot washing and an upper part for hand washing. But this is uncertain. In any case, the priests did not wash in the Laver, they washed at it.

As to its spiritual significance, the Laver clearly introduces us to a subject of very great importance to the child of God. It raises the whole question of sin in the life of the believer; and of defilement and its cleansing.

The Meaning of the Laver

Its Position

The Laver was located between the Brazen Altar and the Tabernacle proper. The Altar stood in relation to the Gate of the court and together, as we have seen, they proclaim the person and work of Christ and the great truth of salvation through Him alone. The Laver, however, stood related to the Door into the Holy Place which was the sphere of priestly service. Whatever the Laver stands for it seems to convey the idea of being suitably fitted to serve the living and the true God.

Its Purpose

In addition to its position, its purpose would also seem to suggest this connection. It was specifically for the priestly family, for Aaron and his sons. Before performing the duties of their office, they were required to wash their hands and feet at the Laver.

Judaism and Christianity, for all their similarities, differ at this point, for whereas the former had a priesthood, the latter is a priesthood. Writing in the general epistles (so called because they were written to God's people in general) Peter said, "you are a holy priesthood." (1Pet.2:5) and again, "you are a royal priesthood." (1Pet.2:9)   The former teaches the God-ward and the latter the man-ward aspects of priestly service.

Every believer is gifted in some way to serve God, and many are gifted in a great variety of ways. But the essential moral qualification for Christian service is holiness of life, rather than gift. It follows that the purging of everything that would hinder the perfecting of holiness must be of primary concern to all who engage in the service of God.

Two Cleansings

There is an initial cleansing from the guilt of sin when we first trust Christ. But the Laver speaks of a daily cleansing from the defilement of sin. Both were insisted upon by the Lord in the upper room, on the occasion when He washed the disciples feet.   Peter's oft quoted objection was, "you will never wash my feet", to which the Saviour replied, "if I wash you not, you have no part with me". The preposition 'with' should be noted. It is not here a question of salvation; or of being 'in Christ'.   It is rather a question of service 'for Christ' and of fellowship and communion with Him.

Peter revealed a lack of spiritual intelligence on this point when he said, "not my feet only, but also my hands and my head".   But Jesus responded, making an important distinction, He said, "he that is washed needs not but to wash his feet for he is clean every whit". The figure is of a person who has been to the public baths and has been washed all over, but returning home along a dusty road his feet have become dirty. To be clean every whit he needs only to wash his feet.

There are two aspects to the believer's initial cleansing. The first is judicial and the second moral and both seem to be brought together in the statement, "Let us draw near ... (i) having our hearts sprinkled from an evil conscience, and (ii) our bodies washed with pure water." (Hebs.10:22) In conversion we were delivered from the guilt of sin on the one hand and on the other we experienced the washing of regeneration. (Tit.2:5) Paul reminded the Corinthians, "such were some of you; but you are washed ... " (1Cor.6:11) In each instance the word translated 'washed' is the word used in the upper room for being washed all over.

Altar and Laver

The terms used have led some to identify the Altar and the Laver with these two aspects of the conversion experience. And it has been pointed out that in the day of their consecration the priests were washed all over, presumably at the Laver. But even if the Laver does carry this thought, its primary message seems to point to the need of daily cleansing from the defiling effect of sin in our lives.

Believers have known the initial cleansing that answers to the public bath. But we walk through a defiling world, and even in spite of ourselves we become defiled by what we see and hear and touch and even by what we say. The Laver brings to our notice the provision God has made for the cleansing of such defilement.

In our previous chapter we saw the blood on the Altar, but now we must look at the water in the Laver. The former deals with the guilt of sin and refers to the initial cleansing experienced by the believer at conversion. It is the subject of 1John1:7. which says, "the blood of Jesus Christ, God's Son, cleanseth us from all sin." The latter deals with defilement arising from our daily walk and is the subject of 1John1:9. where we read, "if we confess our sins, He is faithful and just to forgive us our sins, and to cleanse us from all unrighteousness."

Confession

There will be three factors always present in true confession. Firstly, the need to acknowledge our sin for what it is: we must face up to whatever failure there may be in our lives, we must call a spade a spade. Then there is need to turn from that sin. This is where repentance manifests itself. And, finally, the promised forgiveness needs to be claimed by faith, so that we come to rest on the word of God.

Paul wrote of a sanctifying and cleansing "with the washing of water by the word". (Eph.5:26) Evidently, water is used here as a metaphor for the word of God. As we read God's word each day, the Holy Spirit interacting upon that word, reveals to us how and where we have become defiled. Our responsibility now is to deal with that defilement through self-judgement and confession.

In this exercise we are like Aaron and his sons washing their hands and feet at the Laver. The neglect of this provision would have disqualified them from the service of the Tabernacle just as uncleanness still disqualifies from christian service.

The Making of the Laver

Mirrors Surrendered

It is interesting to note how the materials were obtained for the many vessels of the Tabernacle. The brass for the Laver was originally in the form of polished mirrors used by the women in Israel. Glass as such was not yet available for this purpose, instead they used some very highly polished metal, like brass or copper. The women of Israel willingly surrendered their mirrors for the making of the Laver.   The thought behind this seems quite plain.   Others looking at us can make their judgements about our appearance etc., but it is only by looking into a mirror that we can make a personal judgement.

The surrender of the mirrors for the making of the Laver teaches us the need to surrender our personal judgements and opinions to the supreme judgement of the word of God.   Personal judgements, often dictated by unsuspected prejudices, can vary and may bring disharmony among the Lord's people: but there will be one mind and one spirit where the word of God is supreme.

Like all the Tabernacle vessels the Laver speaks of Christ: the living Word of God who is ministered to us in the written word. Since He is the measure of our perfection we need regularly to resort to the Laver, "till we all come....to the measure of the stature of the fullness of Christ". (Eph.4:13) Every failure that mars the reflection of Christ in us must be purged.

Meaningful omissions

That no measurements are recorded for the Laver must also be significant. This important omission may be taken as a timely reminder that no saved sinner while still in this body of humiliation can attain to the perfection of Christ. At the same time we must never lose sight of that perfection as the ultimate goal towards which we are always pressing.

Details about how the Laver was carried through the desert are also omitted. We thank God for whatever knowledge we have of His word; and we rejoice that He has "given to us all things that pertain unto life and godliness." (2Pet.1:3) But those most instructed in the word, are most ready to admit that they are like children paddling at the edge of a great ocean. There is so much we just do not know. These Laver omissions remind us that a due humility is called for when we handle God's word. (See Deut. 29:29.)

The Material of the Laver

Like the Altar in our last chapter the Laver also was made of brass (bronze or copper) which, as we have shown, is the symbol of discipline or of judgement.   Three kinds of discipline affecting believers are brought to our notice in the New Testament

1. Self-discipline 1Cor.11:31,32.

2. Church-discipline 1Cor.5:1-5.

3. Divine-discipline Hebs.12:3-15

The best of these is self-discipline. If we would only judge ourselves, the need for any other kind of judgement would not arise. The washing at the Laver illustrates this principle of self-judgement in the sense that this was something the priests did for themselves.

Self - Judgement

It was just at this point the venerable Noah failed so tradgically towards the end of his life. The judgement of the whole earth had been committed to him, but alas he failed to judge himself. Since we too are prone to err in this important matter, it is pressed upon us over and over again in the New Testament. Paul reminded the Corinthians: "having, therefore, these promises dearly beloved, let us cleanse ourselves of all filthiness of the flesh and spirit, perfecting holiness in the fear of God." (2Cor.7:1)

The same apostle wrote in similar strain to Timothy. "In a great house there are not only vessels of gold and of silver, but also of wood and of earth; and some to honour, and some to dishonour. If a man, therefore, purge himself from these, he shall be a vessel unto honour, sanctified, and fit for the master's use, and prepared unto every good work." (2Tim.2:20,21)

To be like Christ at His coming is the Christian's hope. In view of that, the apostle John insisted that "every man who has this hope in him, purifies himself even as He is pure". (1John 3:3) In practical terms, as we meditate in the scriptures of truth, the Holy Spirit uses those scriptures to search us, to see if there is any evil way in us. Should such be revealed, we must at once judge ourselves and seek the Lord's forgiveness. Unforgiven sin hinders fellowship both with God and with our fellow believers. We must keep short accounts when it is a question of sin in our lives. This is what we mean when we speak of a daily washing at the Laver of God's word.

PART TWO

The Superstructure

Scripture Reference
Exodus 26:15-30
36:20-34

The Superstructure

Having considered the various details of the outer court or quadrangle, the way is now open for us to look at the Tabernacle proper. Entering by the Gate of the court we came first to the Altar and then to the Laver. Proceeding a little further we shall come to the Door into the Holy Place, beyond which, and past the separating Veil, lay the Holiest of all. Although it was in two separate compartments the Tabernacle proper was a single construction.

The superstructure was made up of forty-eight Boards: twenty along each side and six across the rear with one in each rear corner. The entire front was spanned by the Door. Curtains and coverings were then placed over the top, sides and rear. Finally the Veil was put into position and thus the Tabernacle was set up.

One Tabernacle

It is with the superstructure that we are specifically concerned at this point. The forty-eight Boards were each overlaid with gold. Each Board had two tenons or bands which locked into two sockets of silver thus enabling it to stand upright. A series of bars then held the Boards in place and bound them all together to form one Tabernacle. In a later chapter we shall see how the coverings and curtains speak of Christ Personal, but first we must see how the superstructure speaks of Christ Mystical i.e. of Christ and His people.

The Boards   (The History of God's people)

The work of the evangelist may be illustrated in the servants of Moses going out into the forests to hew trees. The axe was laid to the root of the tree until it was brought to lie prostrate in the dust. In much the same way, *before conversion,* we stood in the forests of humanity: until one day the word of God was brought to bear upon us in the power of the Holy Spirit. We too, were humbled, and brought in repentance and faith, to take our place as sinners undone before God.

Next the tree was stripped of all its natural glory, its foliage and its branches, and then it was fashioned into a Board and overlaid with gold. In this we might glimpse ourselves *at conversion.* Stripped of all hope of establishing our own righteousness, we were clothed with the righteousness of God which is through faith in Jesus Christ.   Each board, now overlaid with gold, was then given a place in the superstructure of God's building. In like manner *since conversion* each believer is 'in Christ' as a member of His Body, a member of that church which is growing unto a holy temple in the Lord.

Saul of Tarsus was such a tree. He stood proudly on the hills of his religion, until one day the axe was applied, and he was humbled under the mighty hand of God. But when God breaks it is only in order to remake: and it was then that Saul of Tarsus became a new creature in Christ Jesus. He became 'our beloved brother Paul.' And to varying degrees this has been the experience of all who are truly in Christ.

Besides the Boards, the pillars of the court also speak of those who are 'in Christ' but in a different way. The pillars represent Christians for what they are in themselves and as seen by men. They were not overlaid with gold. The pillars were seen from outside the Tabernacle proper but the Boards could only be seen from within. The Boards portray believers for what they are as God sees them 'in Christ'.

These two ways of looking at believers have their parallel in Christ Himself. The world saw no beauty in Him whereas His own confessed Him, 'the fairest of all the earth beside.' Do not be surprised, warned John, if the world does not recognise you as God's children; remember that it refused to recognise God's Son. (See 1John 3:1.)

The Sockets   (The Security of God's People)

Each Board was then caused to stand upon two silver sockets. The silver from which the sockets were made came from the numbering of the people. (See Ex. 30:11-16.) Each person gave half a shekel as a ransom for his soul. The price was the same for all, the rich did not give more nor the poor less. The half shekel was called an offering unto the Lord to make an atonement.

The ransom price quite clearly anticipated the price that was paid for our redemption by the offering of the body of Jesus Christ once for all. "For we were not redeemed with corruptible things, like silver or gold ... but with the precious blood of Christ". (1Pet.1:18) The Boards resting upon the silver sockets therefore might illustrate the believers standing before God on redemption ground.

While the Boards of the superstructure stood on silver sockets the pillars of the outer quadrangle stood on sockets of brass. Both sets of sockets represent the finished work of Christ, but in two different ways. The former views the cross in terms of a ransom paid whereas the latter views it as a judgement endured. Together they remind us that the work of Calvary is indeed many-sided.

The Blood and the Word

Throughout scripture the 'blood of the Lamb' is closely allied to the 'word of the Lord'. There may even be a suggestion of these two things in the fact that each Board rested upon two sockets of silver. While Israel's safety on the passover night depended on the blood of the slain

Lamb, their assurance rested on the word spoken by the Lord. It was what the Lord had said about the blood that ministered peace to their hearts. He said "When I see the blood, I will pass over you". (Ex.12:13) In essence, our assurance to-day is just the same: it lies in our recognising the eternal significance of the salvation promises of God.

Prophecy is history written in advance. Of the saints, in their conflict with Satan in a day still future, it is recorded that "they overcame him by the blood of the Lamb and by the word of their testimony." (Rev.12:11) The enemy is always busy sowing seeds of doubt in the minds of many who are undoubtedly the Lord's. The key to victory still lies in the atoning blood and in the assuring word.

'By these we all his rage repel'.

The Bars   (The Unity of God's people)

In recent years no subject has been discussed with more fervour throughout Christendom than the question of unity. As a rule the discussion has generated more heat than light. Nevertheless it is to be feared that many have failed to grasp the very great importance the New Testament attaches to the oneness of God's people. Ephesians chapter four is particularly relevant to this subject. There the matter is presented in a three-fold way

1. A Spiritual Reality. Eph.4:3-6.

2. A Practical Goal. Eph.4:1-2.

3. An Ultimate Hope. Eph.4:13.

By the baptism of the Spirit, on the day of Pentecost,   individual believers were formed into one body and thus the mystical body of Christ was brought into being. Believers to-day are made partakers of that baptism at conversion and thus they are incorporated into the Church which is His body. True believers are no longer, therefore, simply a collection of individuals, they are members one of another because they are members together in the body of Christ. The union of husband and wife in the marriage covenant is the earthly parallel to this heavenly union between Christ and His people. It is a bond that has been formed by the Spirit of God.

Our responsibility is to recognise this oneness and to keep it in the bond of peace. We do this by guarding our manner of living. As we seek to walk worthy of our calling, the Holy Spirit produces in us those graces, such as humbleness and gentleness, which are so essential if strife and division are to be avoided. Even in the event of persistent provocation, the Holy Spirit can develop within the trusting heart a spirit of patience and toleration that will enable us to "forbear one another in love". (Eph.4:2)

But 'the unity of the Spirit' will only find its complete expression at the coming again of our Lord Jesus Christ. Only then will the church now in Heaven, and the church still upon earth, be revealed as one church. Only then will we all come "in the unity of the faith, unto the perfect man, unto the measure of the stature of the fullness of Christ." (Eph.4:13)

The Middle Bar

Besides the three sets of five bars there was 'the middle bar in the midst'. (Ex.26:28.) This middle bar apparently passed through the centre of the Boards and reached from end to end. (See Ex. 36:33.) It acted like a lock, and more than anything else bound the Boards together to form one frame. 'The middle bar in the midst' seems to speak of the presence of Christ in the midst of His people.

Is there anything that heightens an awareness of oneness among Christians more than a sense of God's presence in their midst? At the age of twelve Jesus was found in the Temple in the midst of the doctors of the law. At Calvary, two malefactors were crucified with Him and Jesus in the midst. On the first resurection day He appeared to His own in the upper room and stood in the midst of them.

John, the apostle, saw the risen Lord walking in the midst of the churches and later when he was caught up through an open door into heaven, he saw a throne, and in the midst of the throne there stood a Lamb as it had been slain. The simplest expression of the church in its local character is found in Matt.18:20. "Where two or three are gathered together in my Name, there am I in the midst of them." The Lord only has His true place among His people when He is in the midst.

The centrality of Christ is a very practical matter. Not only does it identify Him as the controller of all, but it means that the closer each of us keeps to Him the closer we shall be to each other. The spokes of a wheel always come closer together as they near the hub. This then is how we shall keep the unity of the Spirit in our various churches and fellowships; it is by keeping close to Christ. The fruit of the Spirit will then be expressed in our relationships with one another, and the practical realisation of our essential unity will not be imperilled.

The Coverings and Curtains

Scripture Reference
Exodus 26:1-14
36:19 ; 39:34

The Coverings and Curtains

If the superstructure of the Tabernacle proper points to Christ mystical then the coverings and the curtains bring before us the grace and glory of Christ personal. The inner curtains were of fine twined linen with blue, purple and scarlet. Embroidered upon them were the Cherubim, which are brought before us here for the first time in the Tabernacle.

These linen curtains were in two sets of five, making ten in all. The curtains in each set were bound together by loops of blue, while the two sets were bound together by taches or fasteners of gold. Together they formed the first covering over the Tabernacle proper; and they were visible only from the inside. (See Ex.26:1-6.)

Next came the goats' hair curtains which were eleven in number. They were also made up in two sets. The curtains in each set were looped together and the two sets were then joined by brass fasteners. The goats' hair curtains differed from the curtains of fine twined linen not only in their material, but also in their number and measurement, as well as by the fact that fasteners of brass bound the latter together whereas in the former the fasteners were of gold. (Ex.26:7-13)

Finally came the two coverings. (Ex.26:14) The first was of rams' skins dyed red, and then over all, the outer covering of Badgers' skins. We shall look at each of these curtains and coverings in turn, beginning from the outside.

The Badgers Skins

The Humiliation of Christ

There is some uncertainty about the skin that is referred to as badgers' skin. Some suggest goats' skin and others porpoise skin. Apart from the Tabernacle references the badgers' skin is mentioned in only one other place in scripture "... I shod you with badgers' skin...." (Ez. 16:10) But this reference gives us the clue we need to understand the meaning of the badger skin; it connects the skin with our walk.

When applied to Christ the badgers' skin seems to point to His self-humbling and to His pathway through this world. This view is supported by the fact that the Tabernacle references themselves relate mainly to the transportation of the Tabernacle through the wilderness. Each vessel of the Holy Place was wrapped in badgers' skin and thus it was carried by the pilgrim people.

No Beauty

The immediate impression of the badger skin upon the mind was one of utter unattractiveness. Isaiah the prophet portrayed the man Christ Jesus as having "no form nor comeliness...no beauty that we should desire Him...a man of sorrows, and acquainted with grief." (Isa.53:2,3)

Many have confessed to having held the idea that Christianity was a drab and colourless business, but that was before they became Christians. The change, of course, was in themselves, and the difference may be illustrated in the contrast between the outer covering and the inner curtain of the Tabernacle proper. Viewed from within the Lord Jesus is altogether lovely; He is the chiefest among ten thousand to His people.

There is much inherent danger in trying to make Christ attractive to the carnal mind and to the natural man. For a time, such efforts may appear popular with many people, but their popularity usually proves transient and their seeming success soon melts away. A time came in the wilderness when the children of Israel grew tired of the manna from heaven, so they baked it in mortars, presumably to make it more palatable. This is an exercise that has been repeated many times, but always to no lasting avail. The attractiveness of Christ can only be appreciated by those who have first become new creatures by the miracle of regeneration.

Rams' Skins Dyed Red

The Consecration of Christ

The Old Testament reference to 'the ram of consecration' should be noted at this point. (See Ex.29:26.) It had to do with the consecration of Aaron and his sons to the priesthood. This association between the ram and the idea of consecration can be seen elsewhere in scripture. It was a ram caught in a thicket that Abraham took and offered as an offering of consecration in the stead of Isaac his son. (See Gen.22.)

The rams' skins dyed red, therefore, speak to us of the consecration of our Lord Jesus Christ. The fortieth Psalm is the Psalm of His consecration: there He is heard saying "sacrifice and offering you did not desire; my ears have you opened: burnt offering and sin offering have you not required. Then said I, Lo, I come: in the volume of the book it is written of me, I delight to do your will, O my God: yea, your law is within my heart." (Psa. 40:6,7,8)

The rams' skins dyed red point to the wonderful truth of our Saviour's obedience unto death. It was in the pursuance of the Father's will that

"He took upon Him the form of a servant, ... and became obedient unto death, even the death of the cross." (Phil. 2:8)

Hidden from view

Perhaps the most significant thing about the rams' skin covering is that it was not visible to human view. The fine linen curtains were seen from inside the Holy Place, the goats' hair curtains were seen by those who approached the Holy Place and the outer covering of badger skin was clearly visible to all. But the rams' skin covering was hidden from view. The consecration of Christ was like that; He said to His disciples, "I have meat to eat that you know not of, my meat is to do the will of Him that sent me." (John 4:32)

Consecration is still like that: it involves the yielding of heart and will. It is something that is worked out in the secret place under the eye of God alone. Even before He was publicly accredited, the Father's eye had rested with satisfaction on His Son so that at His baptism the Father could declare "this is my beloved Son in whom I am well pleased." All this is suggested to us by the rams' skins dyed red.

The Goats' Hair Curtains

The Substitution of Christ

When Jesus comes to judge the nations, He will place the sheep on His right hand and the goats on His left. (Matt. 25:32) Clearly the sheep represent those who are blessed and the goats those who are not. The goat seems to represent man by nature; man as a sinner. When applied to Christ it reminds us of how he took the sinner's place and became the sinner's substitute.

Two Goats

But for Israel the goat had a national significance. On the great day of atonement (See Lev.16.) two goats were taken, one for the Lord and the other to become the scapegoat. The Lord's goat was slain and its blood was carried by the High Priest within the veil and sprinkled before and on the mercy-seat. The meaning of this is fairly plain; it speaks to us of the Lord Jesus in His death as "the propitiation (ie. satisfaction) for our sins and not for ours only but for the sins of the whole world." (1John 2:2)

The sins of the people were then ceremoniously confessed over the head of the scapegoat which, in turn, was led away and tethered in a land not inhabited: a striking figure of the Lord Jesus bearing our sins in His own body on the tree. Here then we have the two sides of the Saviour's subsitutionary sacrifice; on the one hand it was a propitiation, a satisfaction Godward, and on the other hand it was an expiation, a bearing away of sin.

The goats' hair curtains also appear to have a numerical significance. They were eleven in number, in contrast to the fine linen curtains which numbered ten. The extra curtain was folded to hang like a pelmet over the entrance to the Holy Place. Having in mind that the goats' hair curtains speak to us of Christ our substitute, the extra curtain positioned as it was seems to typify our right or title to approach into the presence of God. The blood of Jesus has not only satisfied God on account of sin; it has also opened up a way of access into the presence of God.

> "There is a way for man to rise,
> To that sublime abode.
> An offering and a sacrifice..."

The Fine Linen Curtains

The Exaltation of Christ

When the Tabernacle was set up, the fine linen curtains were visible, but only from within the Holy Place. Lifting up their eyes the priests could behold the fine fabric with its beautiful colours and its embroidered Cherubim. What do we see when we look up with the eye of faith?   "We see Jesus... crowned with glory and honour." (Hebs. 2:9)

> Jesus fills our wondering eyes;
> See Him now in glory seated,
> Where our sins no more can rise.

Having already seen the four colours in the Gate and in the Door, and having noted how they signify the four ways in which the four evangelists set forth the person of Christ in the four gospels, we shall not stop to consider them further at this stage.

The Cherubim

In addition to the colours these inner curtains had superimposed upon them the Cherubim. The Cherubim are first brought to our attention in connection with the expulsion of our first parents from the presence of God.   "The Lord God ... placed at the east of the garden of Eden, Cherubim, and a flaming sword which turned every way, to keep the way to the tree of life." (Gen.3:24)

As well as being upon the fine linen curtains the Cherubim were found on the Veil which guarded the way into the Most Holy Place; within which they were also found on the Mercy Seat. All these instances are directly related to the presence of God. The Cherubim were not found outside the Tabernacle proper, not even on the door that led into the

Holy Place. They were not found in the gate nor in the hangings of the outer court. All this would appear to confirm the view that the inner curtains of fine twined linen speak of Christ risen and ascended into heaven. They proclaim that our Saviour is now in the presence of God for us.

In conclusion, attention might again be called to the remarkable contrast between the exterior of the Tabernacle (the badgers' skins) and the interior (the fine linen curtains). The difference illustrates the great divide in men's thoughts of Christ. To the unbelieving there is no beauty that they should desire Him: but to the reverent worshipper He is altogether lovely. The question, basic to every other question is, "what think ye of Christ"?

The Door

Scripture Reference

Exodus 26:36-37

36:37-38

The Door

Having looked first at the outer quadrangle and then having dealt with the superstructure, the coverings and the curtains of the Tabernacle proper, we come now to consider the Door into the Holy Place.

There was only one way into the presence of God and that way was straight and plain. It did not open from the north or the south sides, in which case a person would have entered and turned right or left. But it opened from the east side of the Tabernacle; by the brazen altar, the place of sacrifice; and it followed a straight course from the Gate of the court, through the Door of the Tabernacle proper and on past the Veil into the Holiest of all.

Only One Way

Jesus said, "I am the way, the truth, and the life: no man comes to the Father, but by me." (John 14:6) Here we have the antitype forshadowed in the one and only way into the presence of God in the Tabernacle. But in this way there were three entrances, the Gate, the Door and the Veil. These speak of the grace that is ministered to us through our Lord Jesus Christ, and in particular of the three things that we have through Him according to Romans 5:1,2.

1. PEACE   "Being justified by faith, we have peace with God."

Type. ------- The Gate of the court.

2. PRIVILEGE   "We have access by faith into this grace wherein we stand."

Type ------- The Door into the Holy Place.

3. PROSPECT   "We rejoice in hope of the glory of God."

Type ------- The beautiful Veil.

The Gate of the court speaks of the Lord Jesus by whom we have entered into peace with God; and the Door into the holy place, the same Lord Jesus by whom we have entered into a place of privilege, an estate of grace and favour before God. And then the Veil teaches us that through Him we shall ultimately enter into the Father's house, for His promise is "I will come again and receive you unto myself, that where I am there you may be also." (John 14:3)

The four colours in the gate were also found in the Door, and we shall see them again in the beautiful Veil. We have already seen how they combine to set forth the Lord Jesus in the fullness of His grace and glory. While there are similarities between the Gate and the Door, there are also important differences. We shall call attention to four things distinctive to the Door.

ITS SITUATION

The Door was located between the Gate and the Veil. The Gate takes us back to the time of our conversion when we entered into peace with God through Him who made peace by the blood of His cross. The Veil on the other hand anticipates the Saviour's return and our going to be with Him where He now is. Between those two great markers lies this present age, to which the Door has a particular relevance.

Priesthood

Its meaning becomes easier to grasp if we have in mind that while the Gate was used by the people, the Door was used only by the priests. One of the distinguishing features between Israel in the Old Testament and the church in the New, is that whereas Israel had a priesthood, the church is a priesthood. At conversion believers are made "priests unto God." (Rev.1:6) The New Testament insists upon the truth of 'the priesthood of all believers'.

We are "a holy priesthood to offer up spiritual sacrifices acceptable to God by Jesus Christ." (1 Pet. 2:5) We are also "a royal priesthood to show forth the praises of Him who has called us out of darkness into His marvellous light." (1 Pet.2:9) These two statements emphasise both the Godward and the manward aspects of priesthood.

The essential privilege of priesthood is the privilege of drawing near to God. When Christians assemble together for worship they should see themselves as priests approaching the altar, not to offer sacrifices of sheep or of goats, but of praise and of prayer; spiritual sacrifices acceptable to God by Jesus Christ.

ITS SHAPE

The Gate was twenty cubits wide and five cubits high, but the Door was ten cubits square. Overall their size was the same but their shape was different. What the Gate had in width the Door had in height. The Gate proclaims the scope of the gospel, "whosoever will may come", but the Door tells of the exalted position into which divine grace introduces those who are the Lord's.

The epistle to the Ephesians, more than any other, teaches the present position of privilege into which we have been brought through grace. We are "blessed with all spiritual blessings in heavenly places in Christ." (Eph.1:3) This must be so since all God's blessing is treasured up in Christ and we are in Him. Our enjoyment of that blessing is limited only by our appreciation of Christ.

Besides viewing us as being 'in Christ' this epistle also views us as though we were already in heaven, for Christ is there and again we are in Him. In the meantime two things should be noted: (i) God has foreordained the kind of people we should be while still in this world; "for we are His workmanship, created in Christ Jesus unto good works, which God has before ordained that we should walk in them." (Eph.2:10) and (ii) although not yet in heaven, we can be there in spirit, for through the Lord Jesus we have "access unto the Father." (Eph.2:18)

Our position of privilege as believer priests is therefore, a very large place indeed. We have liberty to draw near to God; to carry everything to Him in prayer. It is our great privilege "to come boldly unto the throne of grace, that we might obtain mercy and find grace to help in time of need." (Hebs.4:16)

ITS   SUPPORT

The four pillars supporting the Gate will again recall to mind the four evangelists who wrote the four gospels. But the Door was supported by five pillars. Without wishing to press this too far, it is an interesting fact that God selected five men to write the New Testament epistles. (Paul, James, Peter, John and Jude.) With some assurance we might say that in the Gate we see Christ humbling Himself to become our Saviour (the view from the gospels), and in the Door we see Christ risen from the dead to become the Head of the Church (the view from the epistles).

When Rachel the wife of Jacob was dying, she named her newly born son, Ben-oni, which means, "son of my sorrow." But Jacob called him Benjamin which means "son of my right hand." The Lord Jesus is seen in the Gate as "the man of sorrows," and in the Door as "the man of God's right hand." "Though we have known Christ after the flesh [the gate], yet now know we Him no more after the flesh" [the door]. (2. Cor. 5:16) The Door speaks of the risen Lord Jesus Christ as He is ministered to us in the epistles of the New Testament.

The Apostles' Doctrine

The first Christians continued stedfastly in the apostles' doctrine which is now contained for us in the apostles' epistles. Some say they just keep to the teachings of Jesus. Some even imply that Paul contradicted Jesus: but far from a dichotomy between them, there is the most perfect harmony. Others seem unable to get beyond the 'acts of the apostles' to the 'doctrine of the apostles'. Where this obtains confusion inevitably results, especially where this is also linked to an inordinate seeking after the miraculous signs of the Apostolic period.

Only in the epistles do we learn the characteristic truth of this age; that Christ risen has become the Head of the Church which is His body and that we who are 'in Christ' are members of His body. The epistles express the peculiar privileges that belong to those who are united to Christ and whose standing is in grace. By neglecting the epistles and especially the church epistles, a great many have remained as "children tossed to and fro, and carried about by every wind of doctrine." (Eph.4:14) We must know our position 'in Christ' if we are to enjoy the privileges that spring from our union with Him.

ITS   SELVAGE

When dealing with the curtains that covered the Tabernacle superstructure we noted that while there were ten fine linen curtains the goats' hair curtains numbered eleven. The additional curtain was folded like an edging or a pelmet, and was left to overhang the Door of the Tabernacle. In addition to that, we noted that the goats' hair curtains speak of the substitutionary death of our Lord Jesus Christ. This selvage above the Door of the Tabernacle, which was always exposed to the view of the approaching priest, was a constant reminder to him of something deeply significant to us. It speaks of the precious blood of Christ, as the only ground of our approach into the presence of God.

The basis, therefore, both of our forgiveness and of our drawing near to God as worshippers is one and the same. It is the blood of Jesus. "Having therefore, brethren, boldness to enter into the holiest by the blood of Jesus, let us draw near with a true heart in full assurance of faith." (Hebs.10:19,20)

PART THREE

The Golden Table

Scripture Reference
Exodus 25:23-30
37:10-16

The Golden Table

In our Tabernacle studies we have now entered through the door into the Holy Place where none but the priests could come. In reality we rejoice in a Saviour who brings us into a near place, a place of fellowship with God, a place of priestly privilege. Jesus died and rose again, not only that our sins might be forgiven, but in addition, that we might be brought near to God. Of course we must have some understanding of 'this grace wherein we stand' before we can enjoy the privileges that belong to our new and exalted position. What these privileges are is suggested to us by the three golden vessels of the Holy Place.

(1) The Golden Table of Showbread

(2) The Golden Lampstand

(3) The Golden Altar of Incense

To begin, there was the Table of Showbread. The very idea of a table introduces the thought of fellowship; in this instance, fellowship with God and with His people. John's purpose in writing his first epistle was "that you might have fellowship with us; and truly our fellowship is with the Father, and with His Son, Jesus Christ." (1John.1:3) We shall look at how the Golden Table was made, how it was spread, and then at how it was enjoyed.

The Table Made   (Exodus 25)

The two materials from which the Table was made are usually taken to stand for the two natures in our Lord Jesus Christ. The Table was made of wood, 'shittim or acacia wood' (v23). The nature of this wood has already been discussed in connection with the altar of brass; but perhaps the most immediate thing to be said about it is that it grew in very dry soil and hence it was found in large quantity in the wilderness. This simple fact may remind us of Isaiah's witness to Christ, "He shall grow up before Him like a tender plant, and like a root out of a dry ground." (Isa. 53:2)

God and Man

But while the Table was made of wood, it was overlaid with gold (v.24). The two materials seem to emphasise the two natures in our Lord Jesus Christ. He always was God and yet He became truly man, without at any stage ceasing to be God. He is God and man in one unique person. Gold, the chiefest of the metals and the emblem of the divine glory, combines with the wood in the Table of Showbread, to speak of one who was "God manifest in flesh." (1 Tim.3:16) In the mystery of His person, proper deity and perfect humanity are so harmonised that we frequently speak of Him as the God-man.

These two natures found in Christ are often seen side by side in the scriptures. For example, we read "unto us a child is born, unto us a son is given." (Isa. 9:6) Note that the child was born whereas the son was given. The former refers to His humanity and the latter to His deity. It has been said that a Saviour who is not quite God is like a bridge that does not quite reach the other side. The man Christ Jesus who is our Saviour is 'God over all, blessed forever'.

The Table had upon it and all around it a border of gold (v.24,25), and this border which encompassed the table was in the form of a crown. A crown, of course, is the symbol of authority and of sovereignty. This crown witnesses to Christ risen from the dead and ascended up on high where He is invested with all authority in heaven and on earth. It focuses on Him as Paul did when he said, "God has highly exalted Him, and given Him a name that is above every name." (Phil2:9) It proclaims Jesus "crowned with glory and honour." (Hebs.2:9) All this is true of Him now in the presence of God; but a day is coming when His glory will be made known publicly; and in that day every knee will bow in recognition of His universal authority.

The Table Spread   (Leviticus 24)

All the details of the spread Table, and there are many, have a spiritual significance; we shall mention only a few. Every Sabbath day the priests placed twelve loaves or cakes on the table. These loaves were baked of fine flour and were spread on the table in two rows of six in each row. (v.5-8) Four details stand out which might profitably claim our attention.

The flour speaks of the person of Christ. Corn, flour and bread, while representing different stages in a total process, all speak of Christ as the food of His people. This is made clear in the sixth chapter of John's gospel where, alluding to the manna in the wilderness, Jesus said, "I am the living bread that came down from heaven." (John 6:51) Conceived of the Holy Ghost and born of the virgin Mary, the Lord of glory assumed our humanity. He was the true bread that came down from heaven. Then the very fineness of the flour - there were no lumps or irregularities about it - might suggest the perfect life of Christ. "Which of you convinces me of sin?" was a question that silenced His accusers.

The baking of the loaves required them to pass through the fire and this might speak of the Lord Jesus in His suffering and death. Finally the loaves were carried into the Holy Place. Here we see, in beautiful type, our Lord Jesus Christ, risen from the dead, now entering, not into holy places made with hands which are only figures of the true, but into heaven itself.

Twelve Loaves

Twelve is the representative number and every Sabbath day twelve loaves were placed on the Table of Showbread. In 'times past' there were the twelve tribes of the children of Israel and in 'these last days' the twelve apostles of the Lamb. The twelve loaves seem to stand for all the people of God. They represent the corporate company in its entirety. Not one of the tribes was unrepresented. Spiritually the loaves point to the truth that it is for us, as our representative, that the Lord Jesus is now in the presence of God.

The Altar of Incense will teach us what our Saviour is doing in heaven to-day: but the Table of Showbread calls attention to the fact of His being there. We do well if we cultivate a consciousness of this great truth that we have before the throne above an Advocate, a Great High Priest. Upon the palms of His hands and upon His heart our names are graven, and not one is missing. Moreover, He took back into heaven something He had not brought out of heaven, for He is now there in manhood. Christ is in the glory to-day as the representative man.

This may be suggested by the two rows of six loaves in each row. Six is the human number, the number of man. It was on the sixth day that man was created. How wonderful to think that the very man who trod the dusty lanes of Galilee, and who was nailed to the cross of shame, is risen from the dead, and has ascended to heaven, to become our representative in the immediate presence of God.

Thou didst tread the earth before us,
Thou didst feel its keenest woe.

The word 'Showbread' literally means 'the bread of faces'. It speaks eloquently of Christ who shows His face in God's presence on behalf of His absent people: He appears there for us. Exodus teaches that the bread was to be always on the Table and Leviticus insists that it was to be before the Lord continually. These references when taken along with the fact that the bread was replaced every Sabbath day surely emphasise that "He ever lives to make intercession for us." (Hebs.7:25) Every day of the week and every hour of the day this ministry is maintained; and believers, who are at all times exposed to temptation, are ever upheld by their great Intercessor.

The Table Enjoyed   (Leviticus 22&24)

It should not be overlooked that the Showbread was placed on the Table that it might be before the Lord. "Every sabbath he shall set it before the Lord continually." (Lev. 24:8) The Father's pleasure in His Son is the chief thing. It is because He can look on Christ that God is able to pardon us. Indeed, it is expressly stated that the three vessels of the Holy Place were 'before the Lord'.

The showbread was on the Table 'before the Lord Ex.40:25.

The Lampstand was lighted 'before the Lord'   Ex40:25.

The incense was on the Golden Altar 'before the Lord' Ex.30:8.

The really great thing to see is that each of these vessels represented something that was first and foremost for God. It is only as we are able to appreicate the degree of Christ's acceptance before God in heaven, that we can grasp the measure of our own acceptance. For we are accepted in the Beloved. (Eph.1:6)

Who could eat

But the bread on the Table eventually became the food of the priests, and none but the priestly family could feast on the Showbread. (See Lev.24:9.) This suggests a very practical side to the Golden Table. Through believing we have been introduced to the privilege of Christian fellowship, sometimes called the communion of saints. But what is Christian fellowship? It is illustrated in the priests of old as they found a common and a satisfying joy in the Showbread.

The essence of Christian fellowship is for believers to find their common joy in Christ. There are two dimensions to true fellowship. On the one hand it is human: John's first epistle was written "that you might have fellowship with us." And then on the other hand it is divine, for John added, "our fellowship is with the Father and with His Son Jesus Christ." (1John 1:3) Fellowship is much more than just a number of people of similar temperament and outlook enjoying happy times together.

Christian fellowship is enjoyed where believers are found sharing, one with another and with the Father, their common portion in Christ. The Father's joy centres in His Son and we need to enter into the Father's thoughts concerning Him. On our part this calls for constant and increasing occupation with Christ. As the Showbread was before the Lord continually so we must have the Lord Jesus before our hearts at all times. (See Psa. 16:8.)

We become occupied with Him as we seek His face in prayer and fill our hands with service for His name. We feast on Him by giving ourselves to His word. The lost art of meditation must be revived until we become like the man "whose delight is in the law of the Lord; and in His law he meditates day and night." (Psa.1:2)

Who could not eat

But the Showbread could only be enjoyed in the Holy Place: and even then some were not permitted to eat. A priest might be suffering a defilement arising perhaps from within himself or even coming from without. Such a defilement, if it were not cleansed, rendered him unfit to enjoy the holy things. (See Lev.22:4-7.)   In the same way, unconfessed sin in the believer's life destroys fellowship with the Lord and with His people. Since God is holy, it is only in the context of true holiness that fellowship with Him can be enjoyed.

The more we value these things the more we shall hunger and thirst after righteousness, and correspondingly we shall   become the more conscious of our capacity to contract defilement.

> Prone to wander Lord I feel it,
> Prone to leave the God I love.

But He has said, "if we confess our sins, He is faithful and just to forgive us our sins, and to cleanse us from all unrighteousness." (1John 1:9) All who are called to the fellowship of God's Son soon discover that holiness of life is a prior requirement for the practical enjoyment of every privilege of the Christian life.

The Golden Lampstand

Scripture Reference
Exodus 25:31-40
37:17-24

The Golden Lampstand

In the Holy Place and directly opposite the Table of Showbread stood the Golden Lampstand. This was a marvellous piece of workmanship: it was beaten out of one piece of gold. The Lampstand could be described as a central shaft from which projected six branches, three on each side. It had seven lamps which contained the oil for the light.

THE LIGHT

Because it is used repeatedly in scripture the figure of light is familiar to us. On the first day of creation week God said, "Let there be light and there was light." The lampstand and the light that shone from it may well have been in the Psalmist's mind when He wrote, "Thy word is a lamp to my feet and a light to my path." (Psa. 119:105) The light seems to signify God's word. It represents Peter's "more sure word of prophecy, unto which you do well that you take heed, as unto a light that shines in a dark place." (2Pet.1:19)

It is interesting to note the place that light had in the Exodus record of Israel's history. In Egypt there was a plague of darkness, a darkness that could be felt. But Israel had light in their dwellings. (See Ex.10:23.) Then the people were guided through the wilderness by the light of the pillar of cloud and of fire (Ex13:21); while in the scripture before us they had the light of the Golden Lampstand in the Tabernacle.

When analysed, it will be seen that these references combine to teach us that they are a happy people indeed who bring the light of God's word to bear upon their homes and their domestic circles; upon their pilgrimage through this world and upon their fellowships and assemblies. God's word is relevant to all the circumstances of our lives; it addresses all the problems faced by us in this modern age.

Inspiration

It should not escape our notice that the oil from which the light had its source is an emblem of the Holy Spirit. The Spirit of God is Himself the source of the sacred scriptures. We believe the Bible to be the inspired word of God, not just in the sense in which a critic might describe an artist's performance as inspired: but we believe in the verbal inspiration of Holy Scripture as originally given. (For a development of this theme, see 2Sam.23:1,2; 2Tim. 3:16; & 2Pet. 1:21.)

Illumination

Now this light, the significance and source of which we have identified, was to illumine both the Lampstand itself and the entire Holy Place. Its primary function was to illumine the Lampstand. It is specifically stated that "the lamps ... may give light over against the face of it." (Ex. 25:37) The light from the lamps revealed the beauty and the detail of the Lampstand itself.

A careful comparison of Ex.25:34 with Ex.25:32,33 will show that a distinction is drawn between the central shaft (sometimes called the lampstand) and the Lampstand in terms of its branches. This distinction highlights again the two views of Christ repeatedly brought before us in the Tabernacle. As already noted, the pillars of the outer court speak of Christ mystical, whereas the gate of the court points to Christ personal. Again, in the Tabernacle proper, the coverings and curtains have Christ personal in view, but it is Christ mystical we see in the superstructure.

The same distinction can be seen here in the Lampstand and its branches.

THE LAMPSTAND   (i) Christ Personal.

In so many ways the Lampstand sets forth the person of our Lord Jesus Christ. *Before it was fashioned* it was gold. Gold, the chiefest of the metals, is the emblem of the Divine glory, and points to our Lord's eternal deity. In a day when pop gospel and modern musicals are debasing the person of our Saviour, and reducing the Lord of glory to the status of a superstar, we must emphasise His essential and eternal deity. To Him the Father said, "Thy throne O God, is forever and ever." (Hebs.1:8)

Careful attention should be paid to *how it was fashioned.* It was beaten. It was not cast in a mould but it was beaten out of one piece of gold. What a lot of beating must have gone into the beating out of this Lampstand of extraordinary detail. The beating calls to our minds the sufferings and the death of Christ. No tongue can tell what beating He endured when "He was wounded for our transgressions, and bruised for our iniquities." (Isa. 53:5) He so suffered that 'His form was marred and His visage scarred'. And, incomprehensible as it may seem, we read that, 'it pleased the Lord to bruise Him'. Well might He say, "behold and see, if any man's sorrow, is like unto my sorrow."

It is a most interesting line of investigation to trace in the typical scriptures the things that were crushed, bruised or broken. These usually lead us to Calvary and to the sufferings endured by our Saviour on the cross.

And then *after it was fashioned* it was carried into the Holy Place. Surely we can see in this a figure of Christ risen from the dead and ascended into heaven. The everlasting doors have lifted up and the King of Glory has entered into the heavenly sanctuary.

THE LAMPSTAND   (ii) Christ Mystical.

But if the Lampstand speaks of Christ Personal it also sets forth Christ Mystical i.e. Christ and His people. Christ is the head of the church, and the church is the body of Christ. The bread in the communion service represents the body of Christ Personal, the Lord's body: the body in which He suffered. (1Cor.11:24) But in the previous chapter the same bread represents the body of Christ Mystical. (1Cor.10:16,17) The mystical body is the body to which we belong who have been united to Christ.

Considered from the standpoint of Christ Mystical, the Lampstand suggests three things the church must never forget.

First there is the thought of *oneness*. The central shaft and the branches were of one piece. This is a reminder of the oneness that exists between Christ and His people. In breaking the bread of the communion service we are proclaiming, not only that we are one with Christ, but that we are one with all who are Christ's.

On the Damascus Road, Saul of Tarsus discovered that in persecuting the Christians he was actually persecuting Christ Himself. Such is the nature of the mystical union between Christ and His people. "He that sanctifies [Christ] and they who are sanctified [believers] are all of one." (Hebs.2:11) Because of this unique bond between Christ and His people we must be exceedingly careful in the attitudes we adopt towards each other lest we should be found fighting against Christ.

A second thought is that of *fruitfulness*. The Lampstand was wonderfully ornamented. On each branch there were three flowers (blossoms) and three knops (buds) together with three bowls in the shape of almonds. Notice the progression and development, first the blossoms, then the buds and finally the bowls like almonds.

Our Lord stressed this idea of developing fruitfulness in His teaching on the branch that abides in the vine. "Every branch that bears fruit He purges it, that it may bring forth more fruit." and again "In this is my father glorified, that you bear much fruit". (John 15:2&8) In his first epistle John also alluded to three stages in spiritual development, (1) little children [the blossoms] (2) young men [the buds] and (3) fathers [the almonds]. (1John 2:12,13)

There were only three bowls in each of the six branches, but there were four in the central shaft. Here we have sameness and yet superiority and supremacy. The difference between the central shaft and the branches points to the preeminence of Christ. Fruit unto holiness can only be at best a relative matter with us, but in Him it was found in fullness and in balance.

Thirdly, there is the thought of *witness*. The Lampstand had seven lamps. The lamp speaks of witness and of testimony. The central shaft had its lamp. Christ Himself is the faithful witness. The branches had their lamps. And so we recall the risen Lord's parting direction to His own, "Ye shall be witnesses unto me." (Acts 1:8) This is still our task, "holding forth the word of life in the midst of a crooked and perverse generation, among whom we shine as lights in the world". (Phil.2:15,16)

IN THE HOLY PLACE

The second function of the light was to illumine the Holy Place. There was no window in the Holy Place, so natural light could not penetrate there; and yet the whole area was aglow with the light that shone from the Golden Lampstand. The Holy Place was the place of priestly privilege, the sphere of priestly service and ministry. Try, if you can, to visualise the priests moving about in the space between the door and the veil. Their every step was taken, walking in the light; and their every task was done under the full blaze of the light that shone from the Golden Lampstand.

Fellowship

If the Table of Showbread speaks of Christian fellowship, then the Lampstand teaches us what that fellowship involves; it involves walking in the light. The apostle John wrote, "if we walk in the light, as He is in the light, we have fellowship one with another". (1John 1:7) In the light that streams from God's word there is guidance adequate for all so that our way may become as "the path of the just that shines more and more unto the perfect day."

"What wilt thou have me to do?" was Saul's inquiry on the Damascus Road. He received the needed guidance by giving attention to the word spoken by the Lord; and the Lord still speaks to His people through His word. It is only by dilligently attending to that word that we shall be able to serve the will of God in our generation, as Saul of Tarsus did in his.

Working and walking in the light is a principle that applies to all who are the Lord's. Imagine the confusion there would have been, had the Lampstand been neglected and the light allowed to go out. How many once thriving fellowships have ended in confusion because one innovative idea after another was allowed to usurp the place that had been reserved for the teaching and preaching of the scriptures. We shall be preserved from such confusion only as we bring the light of God's word to bear upon all our works and ways.

An important priestly ministry was the dressing of the lamps - this was done every evening and every morning. The spiritual meaning of this must be self evident, but we shall withhold comment upon it until we come to the Golden Altar, where we find this ministry allied to another ministry connected with that altar.

The Golden Altar

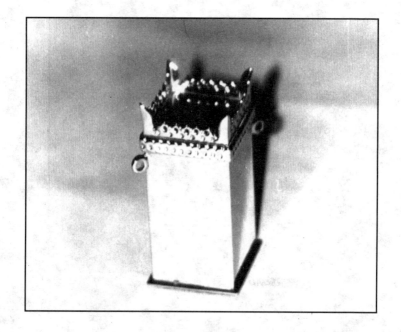

Scripture Reference
Exodus 30:1-10
37:25-28

The Golden Altar

The third vessel in the Holy Place was the Golden Altar which stood immediately before the Veil, beyond which lay the Holiest of all. The very mention of an Altar calls to mind the Brazen Altar, but although the two Altars were in some senses related, they must be carefully distinguished.

The Altar of brass at the gate of the court points to the finished work of Christ at Calvary; whereas the Altar of gold before the veil points to His unfinished work in glory. We have seen in the loaves on the Table of showbread, that He who appeared to put away sin by the sacrifice of Himself, now appears in the presence of God for us. In the Golden Altar we learn what His ministry is as He appears in God's presence. Over this Altar can be written, "He ever lives to make intercession for us." (Hebs.7:25)

Where scripture refers simply to 'the Altar' it is the Brazen Altar that is in view; and where attention is called to the Altar we are now considering, it is always identified by some qualifying word. There are three main identifying terms, and around them the teaching of this Altar may be gathered.

(1) The Golden Altar

(2) The Altar before the Lord

(3) The Altar of Incense

The Golden Altar

Looked at simply as the Golden Altar there are five things to which attention might be called. It was made of wood and overlaid with gold, and it had round about the top of it a crown and upon the corners of it were four horns. It also had two rings for its staves.

We have already seen the meaning of the first three of these items in the Table of showbread. The wood speaks of Christ's humanity and teaches us that there is even now a glorified man at God's right hand. Since this was not so in any previous age, it marks off this present age as being quite unique. The gold points to the deity of Christ, He is the God/man Redeemer; and the crown speaks of His authority. The once slain lamb now stands in the midst of the throne, invested with all authority in heaven and on earth.

The Four Horns

The horn was first brought to our notice in the Brazen Altar. There we gave a number of reasons for identifying it as a symbol of strength and power. On that basis the four horns on the corners of the Golden Altar seem to point us to the universal sufficiency of Christ. The message of the horns is that He is able to save us to the uttermost; He is able to make all grace abound towards us and He is able to keep us from falling, and to present us faultless before the presence of His glory with exceeding joy. (Jude24)

A fruitful field of study opens up to any who take the trouble to examine the sayings of the risen Christ after His ascension into heaven. To Paul, burdened by his 'thorn in the flesh', He said, "My grace is sufficient for you, my strength is made perfect in weakness." (2Cor.12:9) And the different ways in which He presented Himself to the seven churches in Asia Minor are also very impressive. (See Rev.2&3.) In view of this we too may boldly say, "The Lord is my helper, and I will not fear what man shall do unto me." (Hebs. 13:6)

The Two Rings

It is often assumed that because the Altar of brass had four rings, this Altar was similarily equipped, but it would appear that this was not the case. Rather it is emphasised that the Altar before the veil had just two rings. These were on opposite corners and a little below its crown. (See Ex. 30:4.) The Golden Altar, therefore, was probably carried cornerwise, and it is reasonable to assume that when it was placed in the Holy Place it was also in a cornerwise position.

If this inference is correct, it means that the four horns must have pointed directly North, South, East and West. That is certainly how the tribes were encamped in relation to the Tabernacle - there were three tribes on each side. The lesson seems to be that the resources of our Great High Priest are available to each of His people all of the time. The man in the glory ever lives to make intercession for us and ne'er forgets the least.

The Altar Before the Lord

The nearest a priest might approach to God was to come to the Golden Altar, save on one annual occasion when the High Priest alone entered within the veil. That was on the great day of atonement. (See Lev. 16.) But even then the High Priest came first to the Golden Altar. His routine was as follows, at the Brazen Altar he received the blood of sacrifice, then proceeding to the Holy Place he sprinkled with blood the horns of the Golden Altar, after which he passed within the veil into the Holiest of all where he sprinkled the blood seven times before and on the Mercy-Seat.

If therefore, a priest was drawing near or a high priest was entering into the Holiest, all approach to God was by way of the Golden Altar. By the same token, it is by Him of whom the Altar speaks that we draw near to God when we come as believer-priests to offer our spiritual sacrifices.

Spiritual Sacrifices

Principle among the sacrifices we offer are, prayer, praise and worship. There is much confusion about these things and especially about the third, which is the highest exercise in which a Christian can be engaged. We might helpfully think of them like this: prayer is an exercise in which we are occupied with our need, whatever the need of the moment might be; praise is when we are occupied with the supply of our need; and worship is when we are occupied with God Himself. "My God (worship) shall supply (praise) all your need (prayer)." (Phil.4:19)

To varying degrees, we may all be conscious of need, yet only one in ten enters truly into the meaning of praise. (See the miracle of the cleansing of the lepers.) But how few there are who rise to the level of worship. "The true worshippers shall worship the Father in Spirit and in truth; for the Father seeks such to worship Him". (John 4:23) There can never be real growth in grace or increase in the knowledge of God, until we take the shoes from off our feet and find our true place as reverent worshippers before the God of our salvation.

Approaching God

And so the Golden Altar represents another of the great privileges purchased for us by the Saviour's blood; the privilege of approach to God. The tone of our prayer meetings and of our communion services would be profoundly improved if we were careful to offer to God the sacrifice of worship as well as of praise and prayer.

Of course, Christians must see the giving of their substance to the Lord and above all the giving of their bodies to Him, in terms of spiritual sacrifice as well. We are told to "present our bodies a living sacrifice, holy, acceptable unto God, which is our reasonable service." (Rom. 12:1)

The Altar of Incense

One of the daily ministrations of priesthood was the burning of incense. The priest would bring a golden censer full of incense and take fire from off the Brazen Altar; after that he would proceed to the Golden Altar where he placed fire under the incense. The incense thus burned filled the Holy Place with its perfume.

When Mary anointed the body of Jesus six days before He died, she broke a box of spikenard and the house was filled with the odour of the ointment. In Solomon's song we read, "Thy name is as ointment poured forth". (S.of S.1:3) It will not have escaped the attention of even the casual reader of the New Testament that our approach to God is always and only in the name of Jesus. He said, "whatsoever you shall ask the Father in my name He will give it you. Hitherto you have asked nothing in my name: ask, and you shall receive that your joy may be full". (John 16:23,24)

Important light is cast on this matter in Rev.8:3. The 'angel' in this verse seems to be none other than our Great High Priest. He is seen first at the Brazen Altar, where He takes a living flame, and then proceeding to the Golden Altar He takes incense and puts fire under it. As the incense burns its fragrance fills the place and in that fragrance He offers the prayers of the saints.

When We Pray

It would appear that when we pray in the will of God, our prayers are received in heaven by our Great High Priest who in turn presents them before the throne in all the fragrance of His own most precious name. The defects in our supplications are thus overcome and they become a sweet savour to God in the name of Jesus. We dare not approach God in our own name, nor indeed in any other name, but only in the name of Jesus, the name that is above all names.

Jesus, Oh how sweet the name,
Jesus, every day the same;
Jesus, let all saints proclaim,
His worthy praise forever.

The incense itself was composed of three spices to which frankincense was added. More than once it is said to have been sweet. Did John Newton have this in his mind when he wrote, "How sweet the name of Jesus sounds in a believer's ear?" Imitation of the incense was forbidden: "you shall not make to yourselves according to the composition of it". Truly, the name of Jesus is unique and "there is no other name under heaven given among men, whereby we must be saved." (Acts 4:12)

Of the various ingredients, there was of each 'a like weight'. What perfect balance there was in Christ. Judgement and mercy were perfectly balanced in Him. He was full of grace and truth. (John 1:14) Some of the ingredients were beaten very small. It was not just on the big occasions, such as the feeding of the five thousand, but in the small and intimate details of our Lord's life that all the graces shone forth in due proportion.

Morning and Evening

In conclusion it should be noted that the incense was burned twice each day: every morning and every evening. Moreover this was done in conjunction with the trimming of the lamps. (See Ex. 30:7,8.) We have already shown that the light from the lamps represents the light that shines from God's word. Here are two ministries that are intimately linked, the word of God and prayer. Every day, morning and evening, the lamps were trimmed and the incense was burned.

The Christian must pay due regard to these things; at the opening of each day, as well as at its close. We should cultivate a regular habit of speaking to the Lord and of listening while He speaks to us, before we are exposed to the babble of voices that will clamour for our attention throughout the day. And then at its close to speak to Him and allow Him to speak peace to our souls ere we lie down to rest. The neglect of the morning and evening sacrifice incurs a heavy price in terms of our spiritual health.

PART FOUR

The Veil

Scripture Reference
Exodus 26:31-33
36:35-36

The Veil

The beautiful Veil with its blue, purple and scarlet colours, and the Cherubim, all superimposed on the basic white fabric of fine twined linen, is now to engage our attention.

The details of the Veil relate it both by comparison and by contrast to the other entrances already considered. Its size and shape were the same as the Door, but it differed from the Door in that it was suspended, not upon five pillars but upon four. In this it corresponded to the Gate which was also hung upon four pillars; but the Veil was square whereas the Gate was oblong.

Again it was different from both the Gate and the Door in that the Veil was the only entrance to be embroidered with the Cherubim. The four pillars and the four colours would seem to have the same significance in the Veil as they have in the Gate of the court.

We have already seen the Cherubim in the curtains of the Holy Place, now we see them again, this time embroidered on the beautiful Veil. Apart from noticing once more that scripture usually connects the Cherubim with the throne of God we shall leave a consideration of the Cherubim to our next chapter and in the meantime, we shall concentrate on the beautiful Veil itself.

The Meaning of the Veil

(i) The Incarnate Christ

Many details in the Tabernacle may give rise to sincerely held but differing views and interpretations, but there can be no argument about the Veil. In Hebrews we read of "the Veil, that is to say, His flesh." (Hebs.10:20) It would appear that the word 'flesh' is always used in its ordinary meaning throughout the epistle to the Hebrews. The Veil then must refer to the incarnate Christ; the everlasting Word who became flesh and dwelt among us.

The Veil stood between the holy place and the holiest of all, the very presence of God. It was through the Veil that man was ushered into God's presence. It points us to Him who came from God that He might bring us to God.

When Christians sin

John, in his first epistle, views the believer as being always in the presence of God. This raises a vital question, what happens when a believer sins? Does it mean that having been once saved he is now lost and needs to be saved all over again? The answer to that question is an emphatic no. But such an event does give opportunity to the Accuser to slander the failing believer before God's throne. It is at that point the advocacy of our Saviour comes to our aid. Our Advocate with the Father pleads for us the value of His precious blood, and thus the Accuser's voice is stilled.

(ii) Jesus Christ the Righteous

But who is this Advocate? He is none other than Jesus Christ 'the Righteous'. The Veil speaks of Him then, in this two-fold character; first as the incarnate Christ who came from God that He might bring us to God, and then as Jesus Christ the Righteous who not only brings us to God but who in virtue of His atonement, also maintains us in God's presence.

The fact that the Veil was hidden from the view of the outside world might cause us to think of the hidden life of Christ in the days of His flesh. We are taught that having been tempted in all points like as we are, yet without sin, He is now touched with the feeling of our infirmities. (See Hebs.4:15.) Infirmities are to be distinguished from iniquities: the latter are sins whereas the former are weaknesses. It was in human weakness that our Saviour trod this earth. He voluntarily subjected Himself to every sinless weakness common to us. And as He trod this vale of tears, the holy emotions of His inmost being frequently manifested themselves.

Divine compassion

Seven times we are told that He was moved with compassion. Whether it was when He saw the multitude as sheep without a shepherd, or when He came into contact with individuals in their suffering and affliction, He was moved in the very depths of His being. We prefer to dwell on the love of Christ but righteous indignation was also seen in Him. He could be angry and sin not. He also knew how, both to rejoice with those who rejoiced and to weep with those who wept. It is not for nothing that He was called 'a man of sorrows'.

In the Gospels we read how He groaned within Himself. And in the book of Psalms, more than anywhere else, we glimpse the inner life of the man Christ Jesus. And yet He more than any other had this testimony, 'that He pleased God'. In Him every human emotion was holy, and all were blended together in the most perfect harmony. In us, alas, these emotions are contaminated by sin and self.

The Veil Itself

First and foremost the Veil was the gateway into the presence of God. There are two references to the Veil in the epistle to the Hebrews. The first refers to the unrent Veil (Hebs.9:1-8); the second to the rent Veil (Hebs.10:19,20). Obviously we must place the cross between the two, for the Veil was rent at the precise time of the Saviour's death.

(i) The Unrent Veil (A Barrier)

The unrent Veil presented a barrier between man and God and its significance therefore is not difficult to discern. The priests in the Holy Place performing the service of the Tabernacle could not claim to be in the presence of God because the Veil stood between them. They did not dare approach beyond the Veil on penalty of death. Even the High Priest could only enter through the Veil on one annual occasion and then, not without the blood of sacrifice, lest he die.

But in the Holy Place the priests were very near to the immediate presence of God: we might say, God was only 'a veil away'. When Jesus was here among men God must have seemed very near, for God was in Christ and "in Him dwelt all the fullness of the Godhead bodily." (Col.2:9) Men were filled with amazement and glorified God when they saw His wonderful works and listened to "the gracious words that proceeded out of His mouth." (Luke 4:22)

Conviction

And yet among men the presence of Christ had the effect of emphasising the distance between man and God. Even Simon Peter on the occasion of the great draught of fishes, cried out, "Depart from me for I am a sinful man, O Lord." (Luke 5:8) And at the time of His arrest in the garden the very soldiers who came to arrest Him "went backward, and fell to the ground." (See John 18:1-9.)

This helps to explain why the greatest benefactor this world has ever seen was taken and by wicked hands was nailed to a felons cross. Such is the ignorance that is in man by nature: some may have been attracted to Him for a time, but the presence of the Holy One among them was such a rebuke that in the end they cried, "away with Him, crucify Him. We will not have this man, to reign over us."

There are two primary expressions of the righteousness and holiness of God in scripture. In the Old Testament there is 'the law of Moses' and in the New Testament 'the life of Jesus'. We are not saved from our sins by the life that He lived, for the impeccible life of the Lord Jesus served to simply emphasise man's estrangement from God. It is only by His atoning death that sinners are reconciled, and it was at the precise time of His death that the Veil was rent in two.

(ii) The Rent Veil   (A Gateway)

Its Significance for Israel

The rending of the Veil meant that what had been a barrier now became a gateway. For Israel this signalled the cancellation of the entire Levitical system. It was the deathnell of the Old Covenant which was now ready to pass away. (See Hebs.8:13.) It also meant that the sanctuary was no longer in two parts; the Holy Place and the Holiest of all were now one. The priests, therefore, could no longer enter the Holy Place without at the same time appearing to enter the very presence of God and this was strictly forbidden.

Its Significance for the Church

For us the rending of the Veil means that when believers meet for fellowship, which might answer to the Table of Shewbread, they can claim the Lord's presence with them. When they meet to attend on the word, answering to the Lampstand; or for prayer, praise or worship, answering to the Golden Altar, they can claim the Lord's presence. The

Divine presence is not now localised. The Lord's word to His people to-day is, "Where two or three are gathered together in my name, there am I in the midst of them." (Matt.18:20)

God's centre

Without predjuice to the truth of God's omnipresence, we know that in Old Testament times the presence of God was localised; first in the Tabernacle in the wilderness, and then in the Temple in the land. If an Israelite in the wilderness had been asked, "Where is the presence of God?" he would immediately point to the Tabernacle and to the Holiest of all. An Israelite in the land, if asked the same question, would point to the Temple at Jerusalem.

It was not in every place that sacrifice was to be offered, but in the place where the Lord had chosen to put His name. Ultimately that place was Jerusalem. When the Lord said, "gather my saints together unto me" (Psa. 50:5), it was to Jerusalem they gathered. Three times a year the tribes came up to keep Jehovah's feasts at Jerusalem. Even when exiled in Babylon, Daniel prayed towards Jerusalem for that was the place where the Lord had chosen to put His name.

But the rent Veil also proclaimed something new. It heralded the imminent inauguration of a priestly ministry more excellent than that of Aaron and his successors. It was the harbinger of a better covenant, established upon better promises: a covenant whose mediator is Christ Himself. (See Hebs.8:6.)

In Spirit and in Truth

The woman of Samaria, while acknowledging the Jews' insistence on Jerusalem, ventured to suggest that Samaria was the place where men ought to worship. Our Lord's reply was weighty indeed, He said, "The hour is coming, when ye shall neither in this mountain, nor yet at Jerusalem, worship the Father....but the true worshippers shall worship the Father in Spirit and in truth; for the Father seeks such to worship Him." (John 4:19-24)

On Mars Hill, Paul explained the meaning of this statement when he declared, "the Most High dwells not in temples made with hands." (Acts17:24) In other words, the dwelling place of God upon the earth to-day is not a material structure like the Tabernacle or the Temples of old. It is rather a spiritual house. That spiritual house is the Church which is said to be "an habitation of God through the Spirit." (Eph.2:22) The Church which God indwells by His Spirit is not a sect or a denomination, it is the aggregate of all true believers in the Lord Jesus Christ throughout this present dispensation.

Realising His presence

It is important to understand that God indwells the Church universal by indwelling each individual member of it. This means that an awareness of the Lord's presence is not realised automatically by the mere coming together of believers. His presence will be realised corporately only to that degree in which we are enjoying it individually.

Prior preparation of heart and mind is therefore a matter of practical consequence for each believer as it is for the body corporate. The Jews had their preparation for the Sabbath and we need our preparation for the Lord's Day. Each of us should aim to say with John, "I was in the Spirit on the Lord's Day." (Rev.1:10)

The Rending of the Veil

Of the four evangelists three refer to the actual rending of the Veil at the precise time of the Saviour's death. This event perhaps more than any other eloquently expresses the meaning of that death. Mark tells us that "the Veil of the Temple was rent in twain from the top to the bottom." (Mark 15:38) There may have been differences between the Tabernacle and the Temple Veils, but these are minor and the spiritual significance of both is the same.

From the Top

Notice that the Veil was rent from the top. It was not from the bottom as though the rend had been effected by human hands. We must learn to look beyond the physical aspects of the cross and study what God was doing in the death of His Son. Atonement was not accomplished by the actions of Judas or Pilate, nor by what the soldiers did to Jesus. It was accomplished by what God did, "when He made Him, who knew no sin, to be sin for us, that we might be made the righteousness of God in Him." (2Cor.5:21)

To the Bottom

Again, it is noteworthy that the rend was to the bottom. It was not half rent. A complete rending of the Veil took place. Many will see in this very fact a suggestion of the completeness of the work of Calvary.

When He from His lofty throne,
Stooped to do and die;
All the work was fully done,
Listen to His cry.
It is finished, yes indeed, finished every jot;
Sinner this is all you need, tell me, is it not?

In the Midst

Finally, the Veil was rent in twain. The word literally means, 'in the midst'. The effect was to divide the Veil into two equal parts. The cross of Christ is the great divide. History is divided by it. Times past looked forward, these last days look back and the gaze of both converge in the cross. It also divides humanity. Two others were crucified with Him and these two are representative of all. The lives they had lived were identical but the deaths they died were profoundly different. One died in his sins while the other repented of his sins and died in faith. It was their different attitudes to Christ that made the difference. And to this day the preaching of the cross is foolishness to them who are perishing, but to us who are saved it is the power of God.

In the context of our study however, the rending of the Veil is the great divide between the shadows of the Old Testament and the realities of the New. All the sacrifices in Israel's national calendar found their answer in that one great sacrifice of Christ. The purposes of God have now moved forward into a new dispensation in which they are connected, not with Israel nationally but with the Church which is His body: the Church of the firstborn ones who are being gathered out of all nations through the preaching of the gospel of God's grace in Christ.

The Ark (No.1)

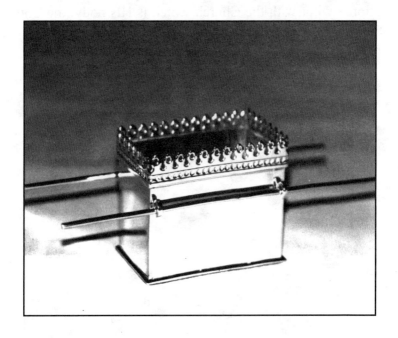

Scripture Reference
Exodus 37:1-5
25:10-16

The Ark (No.1)

The vessels of the Holiest of All were three in number; the Ark, the Mercy Seat and the Cherubim. In a sense there was just one vessel since the Cherubim and the Mercy Seat were beaten out of one piece and the Mercy Seat really formed the lid of the Ark. Nevertheless we must consider them separately if we are to arrive at a true understanding of what they represent. Common to them all is the basic thought that they are vessels connected with the presence of God.

The first vessel in the Court of the Tabernacle was the Brazen Altar which, as we have seen, speaks of the finished work of Christ on Calvary. The last vessel in the Holy Place was the Golden Altar and it speaks of the unfinished work of Christ in Glory. Now in the Holiest of All, we are face to face with the Ark of the Covenant which may be thought of as the chief vessel of the sanctuary.

The Altar and the Ark

It is important to see that, while both Altars speak of the work of Christ, in the past and in the present, the Ark speaks of the person of Christ: Who He is, rather than what He has done. Of course the person and work of Christ are indivisible. Besides their main emphasis we have also seen His person in the Altars and in the same way we can see His work in the Ark, especially in its blood-stained lid, called the Mercy Seat. Moreover the ultimate reality is that His work derives its value from the uniqueness of His person.

The Ark was made of wood, it was overlaid with gold and it had a border around it in the form of a crown. The significance of these things we have already noted when considering the Golden Table and the Golden Altar. They speak respectively of the humanity, the deity and the authority of our Lord Jesus Christ.

The Ark was the first vessel mentioned in all the instructions given to Moses concerning the Tabernacle. Indeed the impression could be received that the Ark was made to contain the Tables of the Law and the Tabernacle itself was made to contain the Ark. It is certainly an interesting study to go through the scriptures and to note the things God puts first.

Christ Pre-eminent

Giving to the Ark the chief place in the Tabernacle surely reminds us of Paul's insistence, "that in all things He [Jesus] must have the preeminence." (Col. 1:18) 'Jesus first' is a principle written large on the pages of inspiration. Here is the fundamental secret of proving the Lord's will and of realising His presence, either corporately or individually; it is to give proper place to Christ.

The Love of Christ

The Ark had four rings through which the staves passed by which it was carried. The ring of course is the universal symbol of eternal love. In the case of the Ark it is noteworthy that the staves were ever to remain in place. It is expressly stated that they were not to be removed; nor were they removed until the Ark finally found its place in Solomon's Temple, amid scenes that are typical of the millennial rest that is to come.

This prohibition on the removal of the staves might speak of the permanence of the Saviour's love. The rings were always occupied. It is true that Christ loved us when He gave Himself for us. It is also true that His love is just the same to-day. If it were necessary, He would do all over again to-day what He did two thousand years ago, when He loved us and gave Himself for us. Praise God, the death of the cross will never need to be repeated. Yet the fact remains, that there is never a moment when His people are not the objects of His tender love and care. "Having loved His own who were in the world, He loved them unto the end." (John 13:1)

The Glories of Christ

In practical terms the Ark was a chest within which certain items were contained. These were three in number; first the Tables of the Law, then the Golden Pot of Manna and, finally, Aaron's Rod that budded. (See Hebs. 9:4.) In speaking of the glories of Christ we usually view them in a threefold way: namely His personal, moral and official glories.

Personal Glory

Those glories in which He stands alone, His personal glories, seem to be represented in the Tables of the Law. The first tables were broken even before Moses came down from the mount. Their breaking was a reflection of what was happening in the camp of Israel at that time. The people had given themselves over to the idolatrous worship of the golden calf. When responsibility is placed in man's hands there is always failure and God's law is inevitably broken.

But the second tables lay unbroken in the Ark; reminding us of one who could say "thy law is within my heart" and "I delight to do thy will O God." (Psa 40:8) Upon Him the Father could look from heaven and say, "This is my beloved Son, in whom I am well pleased." (Matt.3:17) His personal glories are those which attach to Him as the Beloved Son; a position in which He stands unique and alone.

Moral Glory

The moral glories of Christ are what shone forth as He pursued His pilgrimage here on earth: those virtues that were seen in such perfect balance in one who could pass through this scene without being contaminated by it. The manna was God's provision for the wilderness; it was small, round and white. In its every detail it speaks of the Lord Jesus Christ. The practical import of the memorial omer laid up in the golden pot and placed in the Ark, is that it reminds us of Him who trod this earth before us, and who has left us an example that we should follow in His steps. It is by feasting on Christ as He is seen in the manna that we learn how to walk and to please God. And it is thus that the moral glories of Christ are increasingly expressed in us.

Official Glory

Aaron was the High Priest and the representative of his people. His rod therefore, suggests the official glories of Christ; the glories that attach to Him in virtue of the offices He bears. Following the great rebellion recorded in Numbers16, twelve rods representing the heads of the tribes were laid up overnight before the Lord. In the morning eleven of them were just the same as they had been the night before, but one was different. Aaron's rod budded and blossomed. There was life in Aaron's rod.

In this way God vindicated Aaron and identified him as the man of God's choice and the true representative of his people. The picture is sharply drawn. Here we see Christ in resurrection, we see him as the one who ever lives in the presence of God the Great High Priest and Advocate of His redeemed people.

Glories upon glories are upon our Saviour's head, and these are only feebly anticipated in the contents of the Ark. "There are many other things....which, if they should be written every one, even the world itself could not contain the books that should be written." (John 21:25)

> Ten thousand charms around Him shine,
> But best of all, I know He's mine.

The Ark (No.2)

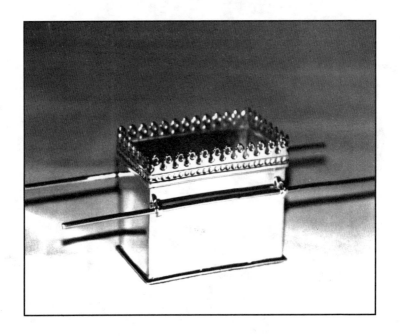

Scripture Reference
Exodus 37:1-5
25:10-16

The Ark (No 2)

All that we have looked at so far, in our consideration of the Ark, is what might be called objective truth; it is mainly on the side of privilege. The history of the journeyings of the Ark shows the other side, the side of responsibility, or the subjective side of things.

The transportation of the Tabernacle was the responsibility of the families of the three sons of Levi; Gershon, Merari and Kohath. The latter had the charge of the vessels of the Holy Place and of the Holiest of All.   This meant that the Ark was the responsibility of the Kohathites.

The Ark in the book of Numbers

It is most interesting to see the order of the tribes when the pilgrimage was resumed following the two years they spent at Sinai. (See Numbers 10.)   Beginning with Judah there were six tribes, then came the Kohathites, followed by the rest of the tribes. Six went before and six followed after with the sons of Kohath in the midst and the Ark of God among them.

Surely the order of their journey and the position of the Ark proclaims the great truth of Jesus in the midst. If 'what it contained' speaks of the glory of Christ then 'where it was carried' tells of His centrality. The Ark was the symbol that God was in the midst of His people. In principle, it is no different to-day, for God is known only where Christ has His place in the midst of His people.

On one notable occasion the Ark was taken from its usual place to go in front of the people, to search out a resting place for them. (See Num.10:33.) This seems to have been as a rebuke to Moses who at that time apparently doubted if God alone was sufficient to be their guide. But even in this the Ark still points to Christ, for "the Ark went before them in the three days journey, to search out a resting place for them." So the Lord Jesus in that three days journey of His death and ressurection, has gone before His people, and is even now preparing a place for them.

The Ark in the book of Joshua

The Passage of Jordan - The Cross of Christ

Three notable occasions involving the Ark of the covenant are referred to in the book of Joshua. At the crossing of Jordan (See Joshua 3), the Ark was set before the people and they were commanded to go after it. Borne on the shoulders of the priests the Ark was brought down into Jordan, then it stood still in the midst of Jordan and finally it was brought up out of Jordan. All this brings the cross before us and speaks of Him who "died for our sins according to the scriptures; and was buried, and who rose again the third day according to the scriptures." (1Cor.15:3,4)

A miracle was wrought when the Ark came into the midst of Jordan, a way was opened up for the people to pass over on dry land. Their going down into Jordan, their going through and their passing over, illustrate the believer's identification with Christ in His death, burial and resurrection. We must recognise that from the time of our conversion, God has viewed us as having died in the death of Christ, and been raised again in His resurrection in order that we might walk with Him in newness of life. Practically, the truth of our identification with Christ must become a recognised principle, governing us in every department of our lives.

At that time the people were told, "when you see the Ark...then...go after it." (Joshua 3:3) In this we are reminded of the exhortation which says, "Let us run the race that is set before us, looking unto Jesus." (Hebs.12:1,2) It is also noteworthy that the Ark not only went down first into Jordan but it came up last out of Jordan. The Ark remained there until all the people had passed over. Christ is the Author of our faith and He is the Finisher of it as well.

Between Ebal and Gerizim - The Coming of Christ

Another notable reference to the Ark is in Joshua 8. Jericho and Ai were now behind them and the people were assembled in the vale of Shechem, which lies between Mount Ebal and Mount Gerizim. With the Ark in the valley, Joshua divided the people into two companies. He put one company on the Mount Ebal side of the Ark and the other on the Mount Girzim side. Then, in the presence of the Ark he held a grand review. The law of Moses was read, the blessings and the cursings, and the whole assembly was exposed to the judgements of God.

This seems to anticipate the coming of Christ when the now divided church will be reunited and we shall be together in the presence of our Lord Jesus Christ. Our lives will then be passed under review and our works will be subjected to the searching judgements of Him whose eyes are as a flame of fire. To live in the light of His coming and of His judgement-seat is a matter of primary responsibility for every Christian. We must occupy for Him now in the power of His Spirit, if in that day we are to have the Master's commendation, the well done of God.

The City of Jericho - The Present Age

Between these two incidents there was another occasion that involved the Ark. (See Joshua 6.) The great battle of Jericho illustrates the Christian's conflict with the world. Throughout the course of this age (which lies between the cross of Christ on the one hand, and His coming again on the other) the Lord's people have proved the Master's saying to be true, "in the world you shall have tribulation."

In our conflict with the world we must be guided, as Joshua and his people were guided, by God's word. Name calling is never a substitute for the power of God, and the Israelites certainly did not overcome Jericho by hurling abuse at its inhabitants. They simply took God at His word and marched around the city. They did this regardless of how much they may have been the objects of derision by the citizens of that place.

To obey God and encompass the city involved two things. First they were to display the Ark and then they were to sound the trumpet. The sound of the trumpet merely called attention to the Ark and speaks to us of testimony to Christ. This is our task as we pass through this world: to call attention to Christ. Our Saviour's parting word to His own was this, "you shall be witnesses unto me." (Acts 1:8)   May we share John Wesley's desire to cry with our latest breath, "Behold the Lamb".

The Ark in the books of Kings

The House of Abinadab

We shall pass over the many lessons thrown up by the history of the Ark as it is found in 1Sam.4-6. These chapters cover a peroid of twenty years when the Ark was hidden in the house of Abinadab on the hill. The present age, during which the Lord Jesus is hidden in Heaven, can be viewed with much profit in the light of these chapters. But we shall turn from all that to consider another notable milestone in the history of the Ark.

The House of Obed-Edom

The time had now come for David to bring the Ark once more into its divinely appointed place. The end was a laudable one but the means employed were not according to the mind of God. Instead of obeying God's word David copied the Philistines. (See 2Sam.6:1-9.) They had transported the Ark on a cart: David went further and had a cart specially built for the purpose. But God had said that the Ark was to be carried on the shoulders of the priests, alas this simple instruction was conveniently ignored.

David's way ended in death. And the Ark, far from being brought into its appointed place was carried aside and lodged in the house of a man called Obed-Edom. (See 2Sam.6:10,11.) It is deeply significant that the blessing of the Lord rested, in a conspicious way, on this man all the time the Ark was in his house. The lesson is fairly clear, if we would know the blessing of God, it will be according to the measure in which we make way for Christ, the heavenly Ark.

The contrast between the house of Abinadab and the house of Obed-Edom is most striking. The Ark had been with the former for twenty years and now as it was being transported, Uzzah presumptuously put forth his hand to steady the Ark when the oxen stumbled. Why did he do it? Was it because after so long a time, he had grown familiar with the holy Ark. We can imagine the reverence with with it was received into the house of Obed-Edom. At any rate the result was most marked; the house of Abinadab was blighted while the house of Obed-Edom was blessed.

The House of the Lord at Jerusalem

If the house of Obed-Edom establishes this principle in regard to family life, the same holds true in assembly life as might be suggested by our concluding reference to the Ark's history. The great Temple of Solomon had been completed save for the final drama, the bringing in of the Ark into its place. When this was done the cloud of glory, the symbol of God's presence, filled the house. (See 2Chron.5.) Whatever overtones we have here of future glory, one practical matter stands out: the experience of the presence of God in the Temple was consequent upon the Ark having its divinely appointed place.

We have seen the Ark 'in the midst' as the people marched through the wilderness. Now in our final reference we learn that Jesus 'in the midst' is the key to blessing within as well as without. Whether considered individually or corporately, in the field or in the house, the people of God must be utterly committed to the centrality of Christ if it is again to be said of a truth, that the shout of a king is among them.

The Mercy Seat and the Cherubim

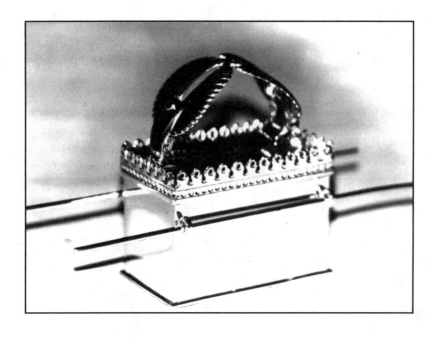

Scripture Reference
Exodus 25:17-22
37:6-9

The Mercy Seat and the Cherubim

The Mercy Seat and the Cherubim which stood at both ends of it, were beaten out of one piece of gold to form the lid of the Ark. We have seen how the Ark speaks of the person of Christ; now we shall see that the Mercy Seat points to His work. The finished work of Christ is highlighted in the Brazen Altar, and the present unfinished work of Christ in glory is seen in the Golden Altar. In the Mercy Seat we shall see the finished work of Christ again, but in a somewhat different way.

The Brazen Altar proclaims the accomplishment of Christ's work when He died on Calvary's cross, whereas the Mercy Seat emphasises the abiding value of that work in the presence of God to-day. This is a matter of very great preciousness: for the Lord Jesus is in Heaven as the freshly slain Lamb. (Rev.5:6)   And His blood is eternally efficacious and can never lose its power. (See 1John 1:7.)

Only One Seat

The Mercy Seat was the only seat in the Tabernacle.   The absence of seats for the priests signified that their work was never done. They offered continually sacrifices which can never take away sins; "but this man, after He had offered one sacrifice for sins for ever sat down on the right hand of God." (Hebs.10:12)

But the Mercy Seat was God's throne. He was known as the God who dwelt between the Cherubim. (See 1Sam.4:4.) Immediately beneath it, and lying within the Ark, were the Tables of the Law, signifying that righteousness is the foundation of God's throne. For a sinner in his sins to approach that throne meant that he must perish. To him it could only be a throne of judgement.

But God had devised a way whereby that throne of judgement could become a throne of grace, a seat of mercy. When Aaron, the representative man, drew near bearing the blood of sacrifice and sprinkled it before and on the Mercy Seat, he did not die. The shed blood had the effect of making that throne a meeting place where a sinner might stand before God and find acceptance.

On and Before

Aaron was careful to sprinkle the blood first on the Mercy Seat, signifying that every claim of God's outraged holiness had thereby been satisfied. Then he sprinkled it before the Mercy Seat signifying that the blood that satisfied God also gives to man a perfect standing before Him. Preachers should make much of the blood shed two thousand years ago, and they should not neglect to stress the abiding value of that blood to-day, for this is the ground of the believer's acceptance before God.

We must always bear in mind that while Israel's Mercy Seat was a place, our Mercy Seat is a person: "Christ Jesus whom God has set forth for a propitiation," the word may be translated, 'mercy seat'. (Rom.3:25) Having, in His life, perfectly fulfilled God's law He was qualified to be the Judge of all. He could have crushed us beneath the law's just sentence. Instead, as our substitute He bore the penalty of our sins, and by His death He accomplished an atonement that qualifies Him to save all who will believe on His name.

Furthermore, when He arose from the dead and ascended up on high, He entered into Heaven, not in virtue of the life He had lived, but in virtue of the death he had died. Even though His death demanded the life He had lived, it is important to note that it was only by His dying that the veil was rent And so by His own blood He entered in to Heaven. (See Hebs.9:12.) His very presence there is witness to the abiding value of His sacrifical death and to our acceptance before God.

Now we see in Christ's acceptance
But the measure of our own.

The Cherubim

Much has been written about the Cherubim and many are the references in scripture to these exalted creatures. They have been called "the guardians of God's throne". They are certainly identified as having a jealous concern for the holiness of God. They are first brought before us in the book of Genesis where, the righteousness of God having been violated, they are seen presiding over man's expulsion from the presence of God. (See Gen. 3.)

In Exodus they are represented as presiding over man's restoration to the presence of God, as from the ends of the Mercy Seat they look towards each other and together gaze upon the sprinkled blood, the divinely established basis of the new relationship. No longer are they occupied with the flaming sword, the messenger of wrath, but their whole attention is upon the peace-speaking blood.

Measurement

The harmony between Christ's person and His work may be reflected in the fact that the measurements of the Ark and of the Mercy Seat were the same. What He did derives its significance from who Christ is. This is a principle of universal application and it is certainly true of Christ. Because He is God and therefore infinite, the value of His work must be infinite as well.

Material

That the Mercy Seat was solely of gold, might indicate the Godward side of the work of the cross, for gold is the emblem of the divine glory. "Christ is the propitiation [i.e. satisfaction] for our sins." (1 John 2:2) When Jesus cried, "It is finished", the sword of divine vengeance was sheathed for God was satisfied. The token and proof of this was His glorious resurrection on the third day.

The Throne of Grace

But then there is another line of truth opened up to us by the Mercy Seat. Believers are encouraged to "come boldly to the throne of grace, that they may obtain mercy, and find grace to help in time of need." (Hebs.4:16) This reference seems to find its parallel in what God said of the Mercy Seat, "there I will commune with you of all things that I will give you in commandment." (Ex. 25:22)

On one celebrated occasion the meaning of this was highlighted in a quite remarkable way. "When Moses was gone into the Tabernacle of the congreation to speak with Him [the Lord], then He heard the voice of one speaking unto him from off the Mercy Seat that was upon the Ark of testimony, from between the two Cherubim." (Num. 7:89) Yet another example of this was when Moses received instructions concerning the various offerings of the Levitical system. "The Lord called unto Moses, and spoke unto him out of the Tabernacle of the congregation." (Lev.1:1)

Thus we learn that the ground of the sinner's acceptance before God, and the ground of the saint's audience with Him is one and the same; it is the precious blood of Christ which is of eternally abiding value in the presence of God. "Having therefore, brethren, boldness to enter into the holiest by the blood of Jesus ... let us draw near with a true heart, in full assurance of faith." (Hebs. 10:19-22)

PART FIVE

How the Tabernacle was Made

Even as we have been considering the Tabernacle proper and the outer quadrangle and all their related vessels, the thought must have arisen in our minds, that the construction of this house of God must have been a very curious work of art. More than ordinary skill was required to translate into reality the pattern shown to Moses on the mount. To appreciate this marvellous piece of workmanship we need to consider it from three different passages of scripture.

How the Materials were furnished   (Ex.25)

Recognising the need

The variety of the materials required for the Tabernacle is the thing that strikes us first of all in this chapter. (See Ex.25:3-7.) Minerals, metals and materials [fabrics] were all needed. This might remind us of the entire field of Christian service where every spiritual gift can find expression and fulfilment. As in the human body every member has a role to play, so in the body of Christ no member is superfluous. There is a service for each of us to render and usually that service is the work that lies immediately to our hand.

The whole creation proclaims that God is a God of variety. Consider the amazing diversity in the landscape with its hills and valleys, mountains and plains, rivers and lakes. In both the animal and vegetable kingdoms we are overwhelmed by the abundance of species, each after its kind.

The great variety of background, temperament and outlook within the human family calls for a corresponding variety in those who are charged with the task of bearing witness to Christ. We are called simply to be ourselves and to exercise the gifts God has given us: in this way we will be used to reach some who otherwise might not be reached with the gospel.

Meeting the need

How the need was supplied also teaches important lessons. Everything was met by the freewill offerings of the Lord's people. (v.2) The giving was not left to a few, for everyone had a contribution to make. There was, however, no force or compulsion, for the giving was entirely voluntary. Above all, the offerings were given lovingly. "Of every man that gives it willingly with his heart you shall take my offering."

This is still the principle that is to govern us to-day. Whatever may be given in the service of God, be it in time, talents or substance, shall have the approbation of God in that day, only if what is given is rendered out of a heart that is constrained by the love of Christ.

In the presence of pressing need Paul wrote to the Corinthians for help. (See 2nd Cor.8.) In his appeal he used the churches of Macedonia by way of example. "This they did, not as we had hoped, but first gave themselves to the Lord, and then to us by the will of God." The materials God uses and in which He takes pleasure are those given by people who have first given themselves to Him. There is an urgent need, not so much for consecrated gifts, but for consecrated givers.

How the men were fitted   (Exodus 31)

Wisdom from on high

Bezaleel was the chief workman in the construction of the Tabernacle. He had as his first assistant a man called Aholiab. Under them there was a workforce of wise-hearted men. Thank God for the willing-hearted, but Christian service also needs men who are wise-hearted. "Is there not a wise man among you" was Paul's rather sharpe rebuke to the Christians at Corinth. Much heartbreak and mischief has arisen among the people of God by failure at this point.

There is a pressing need for men and woman imbued with 'the wisdom that is from on high'; worldly wisdom will not do. Happily the needed wisdom is available for "if any man lack wisdom, let him ask of God, who gives to all men liberally, and upbraideth not, and it shall be given him." (Jas. 1:5 & 3:13-18)

Attention must also be called to the appointment of Bezaleel. He was divinely called, and his call was both personal and practical. He was called by name (v.1) and he was called to work. (v.5) We too have been called to work, to serve God acceptably, with reverence and godly fear. After Paul came to know the Lord, his first concern was to know God's will. He said, "Lord, what wilt thou have me to do?" (Acts 9:6) It is given to us first to know the will of God and then to do it with all our might.

Filled with the Spirit

This brings us to the important matter of the chief workman's equipment, for when God calls He always equips. The workman needed wisdom and understanding as well as knowledge. All these he was given in conjunction with the Spirit. "I have filled him with my Spirit" was God's word to Moses. Nothing was given independently of the Spirit. Deprived of the Spirit's power Bezaleel would have become like any other man. No matter what Christian service we may engage in, "it is not by might, nor by power, but by my Spirit, saith the Lord of Hosts." (Zech. 4:6)

To be filled with the Spirit is the best, and in the end, the only equipment a person needs to serve the living and the true God. No man should consider himself fit for the service of God so long as there is upon his conscience something that is grieving or quenching the Holy Spirit. The Spirit filled life is a life of effective service.

Ultimate purpose

Bezaleel's assignment is also worthy of note. He was to devise cunning works, to work in gold, in silver and in brass. He was also engaged in the cutting and setting of stones and in the carving of timber. He was more than just a quarryman for he was responsible for the ultimate use and purpose of each stone. Nor was he merely a hatchet man, procuring timber by cutting down trees. He had an ultimate purpose in view at all times.

Paul laboured much for the conversion of sinners, but he always had in view God's ultimate purpose for those who are saved. His aim was to "present every man perfect in Christ Jesus." (Col.1:28) Every mother looks for growth and development in her children and the Lord looks for maturity in all who profess His name. Our aim should be that we might be helpers one of another towards the great goal of ultimate conformity to Christ.

How the matter was finished   (Ex 40)

Count the number of times the commandment of the Lord is referred to in this chapter. "As the Lord commanded Moses, so did he." Subjection to the Lord and obedience to His word were the things that governed Moses in bringing this mighty enterprise to such a successful conclusion. Nothing was left to speculation or conjecture. All was governed by the word spoken to Moses and all was according to the pattern shown him on the mount.

The Tabernacle set up

This last chapter of Exodus begins with a reference to the calendar, to the first day of the first month. (v.2) This of course was the date of the passover which speaks to us of the cross. The rearing up of the Tabernacle on that day seems to emphasise the fact that everything that is of God has been established on the ground of redemption. It might also speak to us of the time of our coming to faith in Christ for that marked the beginning of our spiritual experience.

Now add to that the fact that the chapter ends with a reference to the cloud, the symbol of the Lord's presence with His people. "The cloud of the Lord was upon the Tabernacle by day, and the fire was on it by night, in the sight of all the house of Israel, throughout all their journeys." (v.38) There never was a time when they were without the presence of the pillar of cloud and of fire. And "so Moses finished the work." (v.33)

And what a finish! A redeemed people, enjoying an awareness of the Lord's presence with them, carried the work to its conclusion in a spirit of subjection to the Lord and of obedience to His word. "I have finished the course", was the apostle Paul's triumphant farewell. He too was marked by that same spirit of humble subjection and ready obedience to the revealed will of God. May such be our distinguishing mark as well.

How the Tabernacle was Moved

The children of Israel in the wilderness were a nomadic people, moving about from place to place. Repeatedly they pitched and they encamped for there they had no continuing city. This meant that the Tabernacle had to be frequently dismantled, transported and then set up again in another location. Very detailed instructions were given to govern this operation so that, even in this matter, the people might have the Lord's mind to guide them.

Our purpose is to take a broad overview of the moving of the Tabernacle and to glean some spiritual lessons from it even though it will mean setting aside a great deal of very significant detail.

The Firstborn

On the occasion of the passover night in Egypt, the firstborn was redeemed by the blood of the slain lamb. Thereafter, God claimed the firstborn of man and of beast for Himself. For example, He said to Moses, "every firstling of an ass shalt thou redeem with a lamb; and if thou wilt not redeem it, then thou shalt break its neck; and all the firstborn of man among thy children shalt thou redeem." (Ex.13:13)

Later in the plains of Sinai where Israel had tarried for two whole years, instead of taking the firstborn of every family of every tribe throughout the nation, the Lord chose the entire tribe of Levi. "Bring the tribe of

Levi near, He said, to do the service of the Tabernacle", and again, "the Levites shall be mine." (Num. 8:14) Thus the Levites were set apart to do the service of the Tabernacle. This included all that was involved in its being moved from place to place.

In the day of their consecration the Levites were presented as an offering to the Lord. They became a living sacrifice. (See Rom. 12:1.) They cleansed themselves by washing their clothes and by shaving their flesh in keeping with the principle, "be ye clean that bear the vessels of the Lord." This was a practical cleansing and a reminder that we too must subject our lives to 'the washing of water by the word' and we too must apply to ourselves the sharp razor of self-discipline and of self-judgement.

The Tribe of Levi

The Levites were required to devote those years of their lives between 25 and 50 to the service of the Tabernacle. These are the best years of a person's life and would suggest that in its most basic expression, consecration is simply giving of one's best to the Lord.

Although the nation as a whole was numbered from twenty years old and upward, i.e. all who were able to go to war; the Levites were numbered from one month old. The thought seems to be that when it is a matter of responsibility and of defending the inheritance maturity is called for, but when it is a question of privilege, of approach to God, of fellowship and service, the latest believer is on the same ground as the more mature.

Even then, although numbered at one month, it would appear that after entering upon Levitical service at the age of twenty five, they passed through some sort of apprenticeship before assuming their full share of responsibility at thirty.

Three Families

The three families that made up the tribe of Levi were the sons of Gershon, of Merari and of Kohath. Some have seen in their respective duties the three great ministries given to the church by the ascended Lord. "He gave some, evangelists; and some, pastors and teachers." (Eph.4:11)

When the Tabernacle was being transported, the Gershonites had as their burden the outer Court of fine twined linen and the gate. This might represent the Evangelist's burden which is to show men the holiness of God and their unfitness to approach into His presence. His task is also to proclaim that God, in mercy, has provided a way into His presence through the Lord Jesus Christ.

The ministry of the Merarites was to bear the superstructure of the Tabernacle; the boards, the bars, and the middle bar in the midst. Here we have those things that point to Christ mystical, to Christ and the church. It is in this area of Church fellowship, 'endeavouring to keep the unity of the Spirit in the bond of peace' that the Pastor finds scope for the exercise of his peculiar gift.

It was the Kohathites who concentrated on the vessels of the Holy Place and of the Holiest of all. Similiarly it is the duty of the Teacher to instruct the people in the matter of their privileges, privileges most wonderfully set forth in the vessels carried by Kohath. Doubtless, others see the respective duties of the three houses of the tribe of Levi in other lights; but our purpose is to focus on the children of Kohath and the part they had in the service of the Tabernacle.

Picking and Choosing

There appears to have been some room for choice in the work of Gershon and Merari. One might have said of a particular object, "I carried that last time, I'll take something different this time." This was certainly not the case with Kohath. Since he was to carry the vessels of the sanctuary, the High Priest came along first and covered all the vessels with appropriate coverings and then put them into the hands of whoever was to carry them. There was no picking and choosing, each man filled his hands with whatever was committed to him by his High Priest. (See Num.4.)

We are all too familiar with those who lightly take up some aspect of Christian service and lay it down again just as lightly. Better to enquire, "Lord, what wilt thou have me to do" and then to fill our hands with that, for only such service will have the well-done of God at the Judgement-Seat of Christ.

Kohathite Service

The service of the Kohathites in their day was probably viewed as much Christian service is viewed to-day. When the princes of Israel donated six wagons and twelve oxen for the carriage of the Tabernacle, instead of dividing them equally among the three families, Moses gave two wagons and four oxen to Gershon and the rest to Merari. (See Num. 9.) It seemed that Kohath had been overlooked just as to-day when words of praise are spoken, much true service for God passes unnoticed.

But God's way for Kohath was that his burdens were to be borne upon his shoulders. This must have made his work appear unspectacular. Moreover, the burdens themselves must have been unsightly for the various pieces were wrapped in badgers' skins. We can say with confidence that there was nothing outwardly attractive about Kohath's work; in this it also resembles much valuable service for the Lord in our own day.

Again, the service of the Kohathites was relatively inconspicuous because when the people were marching, Gershon and Merari always went first and Kohath invariably brought up the rear. (See Num.10.) Whatever practical reasons there may have been for this, it would appear that the Kohathites were content, in the plan of God, not to occupy the foreground. They were the back room people of their day. Manifestly, a multitude of faithful servants of Christ to-day must see their lot reflected in the service of the sons of Kohath.

Appearance

But all this is judging by outward appearance. The God of the Tabernacle looked beyond the outward, beyond the badger's skin; He saw that the burden Kohath carried was pure gold. He saw the Golden Lampstand and the Golden Table etc.

Christian service will be reviewed at the Judgement-Seat of Christ, not to establish the size of it, but the sort of it. (1Cor. 3:13) Our service does not have to be prominent or spectacular to be pure gold in the Lord's eyes. But like the service of Kohath, it must be wrought in complete subjection to our Great High Priest.

"Therefore, my beloved brethren, be steadfast, unmoveable, always abounding in the work of the Lord, forasmuch as you know that your labour is not in vain in the Lord." (1Cor.15:58)